La Música de los Viejitos

La Música de los Viejitos

Hispano Folk Music of the Río Grande del Norte

Jack Loeffler

with

Katherine Loeffler &

Enrique R. Lamadrid, Ph.D.

Photography by Jack Parsons

UNIVERSITY OF NEW MEXICO PRESS / ALBUQUERQUE

This work is dedicated to
la gente del Río Grande del norte.

Library of Congress Cataloging-in-Publication Data
applied for.

In the recordings on the accompanying compact discs,
some long selections were edited.
Those selections appear in the text in their entirety.

Contents

7 ॐ *Más Cantos, el Teatro, y los Matachines*

Acknowledgments

A GREAT NUMBER OF PEOPLE contributed to the making of this book including the many folk musicians whose work is presented here. I wish to express my heartfelt thanks to everyone who helped including my old and dear friend Lee Udall, whose quiet commitment to the preservation of folklore, folk art, folk music and folk culture has helped ensure the continued presence of indigenous wisdom; my late partner and superpal, Karl Kernberger, with whom I shared myriad adventures into the backcountry of everywhere; the late John D. Robb, friend, mentor, and pioneer; John Depuy, friend, artist, and madman, who introduced me to the very first Hispano folk musician I ever recorded; the late Ed Abbey, mi hermano y compañero, who relentlessly urged me on and ever lauded and supported the salt of the Earth; Beth Hadas, Barbara Guth, Liz Varnedoe, and especially my friend Emmy Ezzell of the University of New Mexico Press; Bernie López, the late Mike Jenkinson, John Vincent, Tisa Gabriel, the late Peggy Weafer, and Eleanor Broh-Kahn, all formerly with the New Mexico Arts Division and all committed to helping the artist rather than advancing bureaucracy for its own sake. Without their support this project could not have happened.

Bess Lomax Hawes and Dan Sheehy from the National Endowment for the Arts, whose grants and spiritual support made all of the field recording for this project possible; Tom O'Connor and Suzanne Jameson, who helped me secure funding to pursue ever more field recording and radio production; John Hill, who introduced us to Vicente Montoya and Margarito Olivas; George Ewing and Charlene Czerny, who provided a haven and a venue for folk festivals when others abandoned ship; Celestia Peregrina Loeffler who attended many recording sessions.

And my many friends along the way including Tom Dickerson, Tony Mares, Jimmy Leger, Joe Wilson, Claude Stephenson, Jim Wright, Charlie Maude Curtis, Rowena Rivera, Charlie Carrillo, Owen López, Gregorita Rodríguez, Willie Apodaca, Gary Snyder, Alex and Virginia Chávez, Will Wroth, Chuy Martínez, Dana Everts, Alan Jabour, Landon Young, Fred Steiner, Jillian Sandrock, Peter Mattair, Charlie Seemans, Elaine Thatcher, Howard Bass, Tony Isaacs, Susan Ohori, Peter Garland, Carl Bernstein, Pat Neher, David Noble, Nancy Uscher, Charles Aguilar, and William Field.

And my extraordinary and beloved wife, Katherine, and my dear friends Enrique R. Lamadrid, Cipriano Vigil, Brenda Romero and Jack Parsons, all of whom actually helped make the book.

Jack Loeffler
Los Caballos
1999

Introduction

Pedro de Gante, a Franciscan friar from Flanders, founded the first school of European music in the New World in Texcoco, Mexico, in 1524. The purpose of this school was to teach Indians liturgical music. Shortly thereafter the Indians were performing church music throughout the area under Spanish dominion.

De Gante, with a dozen Franciscan missionaries, taught the Indians musical notation, Gregorian chant, performance on European instruments, and instrument construction. The Indians learned to fashion wind instruments, drums, and stringed instruments, including the precursors of the modern violin and guitar.

Two years later a man named Ortiz, who is reputed to have been a companion of Cortez and who played the *vihuela,* opened a school of dance in Mexico City. Within a decade of the spectacular conquest of Mexico by Hernán Cortez, the sacred and secular music of Spain had tapped roots into the soil of the Western Hemisphere. Before the close of the sixteenth century, this musical tradition followed the trail of the *Camino Real de Tierra Adentro* northward into the region of the Río Grande del Norte. In 1598, when Juan de Oñate and the Spanish colonists established their settlement at the confluence of the Río Grande and Río Chama, it was to the beat of their own music.

The Spanish colonists of the Río Grande del Norte remained in a state of relative isolation for centuries. During the Pueblo Revolt of 1680, all of the original colonists including the Franciscan priests were either killed or forced to flee. Many returned with de Vargas in 1692 and settled into this harsh and overwhelmingly beautiful environment with an unquestionable finality. They adapted to the land and the land accepted them. The quest for gold that had motivated their forebears had abated, and the colonists became content to match wits with the seasons and survive. Their culture retained vestiges of Renaissance Spain while acquiring a spirit distinctly its own. They coexisted with the Pueblo Indians and there was major cultural overlap. The Hispanos perpetrated a medieval Christian ethos which found its way into the pueblos, but it failed to supplant the local deities who still remain strong in this mythic landscape. The Hispanos, in turn, learned survival skills from the Puebloans and insinuated these skills into their own widening system of coordinates. They grew crops, built churches, hand-crafted their lives with a minimum of metallurgy, hunted game including buffalo, fought off and traded with Apaches, Navajos, Comanches, and Utes, and little by little divested themselves of European authority and evolved within a cultural matrix of their own collective invention. With the passage of generations, their *camposantos,* or cemeteries, rooted them to the land that they had come to know with great intimacy. The Spanish villages flourished in a fashion corresponding to the flow of Nature. The *acequias,* or irrigation canals, became the focus of local politics beyond which few cared to stray.

And throughout this period they socialized, and for every event there was music. For every mood from poignant introspection to spiritual affirmation, to the recounting of lore, to the beat of the dance, there was music. There was music from antiquity and music from the constantly changing present. Over a span of nearly half a millennium, a vast musical heritage accompanied the passage of Hispano generations. Currently, only fragments of it can be perceived.

Memory is ephemeral, and only faint echoes of this musical heritage still pass across the face of the land. The work of earlier lore collectors such as Espinosa, Rael, Campa, Lucero, Cobos, and Robb describes a richness that has largely faded. However, the trove is far from depleted, and the region of the Río Grande del Norte yields music that spans centuries and reflects points of view and recollections that have otherwise disappeared.

Within the context of their traditions, folk musicians are rarely regarded as professional performers, although they may accept money or goods for performing. Generally they work at other kinds of labor for their sustenance. Until the last generation or two, most of *la gente* in the region of the Río Grande del Norte relied to some extent on farming, raising livestock, hunting, and trading. Money was a rare commodity. Since World War II, many of the men have taken jobs as laborers or municipal, state, or federal employees. Cities like Santa Fe, Albuquerque, and Los Angeles have enticed others who in earlier times might have spent their lives in a more rural environment. Even so, many of the small, traditional communities have remained relatively intact. Relative, that is, to the presence of the automobile, electricity, and media.

Most of the folk musicians presented here have led normal lives within the context of Hispano culture but have distinguished themselves by their musical talents. They have contributed greatly to the realm of *Nuevo Mexicano* musical tradition, and it is this aspect of their lives with which this work is concerned. They live within an area that extends from La Mesa, New Mexico, just north of the international boundary with Mexico, to the San Luis Valley of southern Colorado, bounded on the east by the Great Plains and on the west by the Continental Divide.

The physical characteristics of this region include the Río Grande del Norte, the Southern Rocky Mountains, arid grassland, and the Chihuahuan Desert. Spanish colonization of the region began in the sixteenth century. The northernmost colonists remained isolated from their southern neighbors because the expanse of land that extended from Qualacu, south of Socorro, to El Paso and beyond is arid and was dominated by hostile Indians.

Consequently *la gente del norte* bear cultural characteristics distinctly their own. The southern part of this region reflects a modern Mexican influence that is equally rich in tradition, and with the advent of accessible modern transportation and media, cultural exchange has accelerated. Therefore the folk music of the Río Grande del Norte often includes songs of Mexican provenance. Music, like a flock of birds, is not contained by political boundaries.

World War II was a landmark for *Nuevo Mexicanos*. A disproportionately high number of Hispano men were conscripted into the U.S. armed forces. Most of these men were sent to wage war against the Japanese in the South Pacific, where many of them were killed. Indeed the Bataan Death March tolled the final knell for many of these men, and their loss was felt personally as well as culturally. Those who did survive returned to their own milieu, where the pace of change hastened. The social, cultural, and economic transformations in Hispano society were reflected in its music.

One characteristic of folk music is that it is passed from musician to musician through oral tradition. The *Encyclopaedia Britannica* defines oral tradition as "the aggregate of customs, beliefs, and practices that were not originally committed to writing, but contribute to the cultural continuity of a social group and help shape its views." Since folk music notation, whether vocal or instrumental, is rarely written down, each performance is subject to varying degrees of recollection, technical expertise, interpretation, and style. No piece is performed exactly the same way twice. Therefore each piece that gains prominence inevitably goes through myriad permutations.

Many of the *músicos* have books, or *cancioneros,* in which they write the lyrics to the songs in their repertoires. In comparing different versions of a song, differences in the lyrics become evident.

In the present work, each of the folk songs appears on compact disc and in transcribed form. The transcribed musical notation corresponds to the melody as it was played the first time through. The listener who compares the musical transcription with the CD will note that the repeated melody lines frequently vary. This is the nature of folk music performance. In some instances it is difficult to discern precisely what notes are being played or what words are being sung. The Spanish lyrics and their English translations are included in their entirety. It is possible to compare many of these songs with versions that appear in other works to discover different regional styles. The photographs portray the *músicos* within their milieu and convey the character of their everyday lives.

It is difficult to describe how a dance is performed; we include both verbal descriptions and graphic illustrations of dance technique. The method we have devised will allow anyone who reads music to know where the foot falls relative to the musical beat and how the dancers' bodies are positioned at any given point in the music.

The music included here spans centuries; however, a large proportion of it has become prominent only in the last 150 years. Many musical forms that prevailed in earlier times have disappeared, and we can only imagine how the music sounded. Even some of the forms in this book are now moribund, and this work is intended in part to celebrate their passage. The *décima,* formerly an important poetic musical form, is now all but extinct in this region. Few recall the *romances,* or narrative ballads, born on the Spanish peninsula, and *relaciones* also reflect the spirit of a time that has passed.

However, it remains astonishing that this rich musical tradition exists to the degree that it does. The music wanders through the labyrinth of human emotional experience, and the tradition continues as new songs are composed to old forms. In the case of *nueva canción,* the "new song" movement that has recently swept the hemisphere, a new form is evolving within the context of the tradition. It is occasionally possible to trace the passage of the musical baton from one generation to the next–both the pleasure and the pain of it.

Sometimes there is a raw quality to the sound of folk music. This rawness reflects a handcrafted way of life. Elderly Hispano folk musicians often express a deep level of spiritual refinement. Folk music belongs to those who live at the grassroots of existence and who are able to spontaneously express their feelings through it. Music is their solace and their joy.

The songs and melodies selected for this work are representative of the musical forms found in Hispano culture in the region of the Río Grande del Norte. This folk music was traditionally sung and performed on instruments fashioned in a time before electrical amplification. The music expresses the heart of Hispano culture as perceived by an older generation whose memories reflect a mosaic of change. It is our belief that many older people, the elders of a culture, recall their lifetimes in nonlinear fashion, perceiving the totality of their individual and collective existences by recalling clusters of experience related by the emotional responses they elicit rather than the moment in time at which they occurred. It is true that in many narrative ballads called *corridos,* the day, month, and year are included in the *versos,* thus establishing an intellectual decree that demands some accuracy within the oral history. But in the main, it is another attribute that sustains the culture, something more soulful, heartfelt, and emotional, intuited in a fashion much more encompassing than the deductive processes.

Whereas urbanized Americans are accustomed to being driven by the clock, many rural residents of the Southwest still think in terms of the position of the sun or the passage of the seasons. To a great extent it is the habitat that dictates, rather than the human being. Everyone should note that in the arid Southwest, the human population cannot exceed the carrying capacity of the watershed for long before disaster ensues. Here cultural diversity and bioregional diversity are intricately intertwined. Subsisting harmoniously within the flow of Nature has been found to be compatible with survival, and thus cultures evolved in cooperation with natural forces. It is in this spirit of La Tierra Sagrada, The Sacred Earth, that the *Nuevo Mexicano* people of the rural communities of the Río Grande del Norte continue to pursue their cultural destiny.

CHAPTER ONE

Romances y Relaciones

THE MOUNTAINS AROUND THE RÍO GRANDE DEL NORTE still ring with the echoes of songs first sung hundreds of years ago in Spain, during a time when the acts of men and women were recollected in narrative ballads called *romances*. These ballads sometimes worked their way to the New World in the hearts and minds of *conquistadores* and Spanish colonists, where they remained as oral remnants of a European tradition.

The *romance* form of narrative ballad has its roots in the epic poetry of the twelfth century. It apparently came into its own by the thirteenth century, when the *juglares* (who were wandering acrobats, jugglers, poets, dancers, and musicians) performed in public squares or in the houses of the nobility.

Originally the *romances* were passed down by oral tradition. However, in 1511 an edition entitled *Cancionero General,* assembled by Hernando del Castillo, contained thirty-seven of these ballads, over half of which were by identified authors. The *romances* exalted the deeds of warriors, kings, and the gentry. Therefore they were eagerly listened to by everyone including chroniclers and historians, who regarded them as popular accounts of significant episodes. Traditionally their melodies have thirty-two-note lines, which correspond to the thirty-two-syllable stanzas, in turn comprised of two sixteen-syllable rhymed or assonated verbal lines (*versos*). They were popular in Spain at the time of the conquest and undoubtedly arrived in the New World in the sixteenth century. A few of the old *romances* are still sung by the Hispano folk musicians of New Mexico. They represent a part of the ancient lineage of Spanish vernacular poetry that extends into the twentieth century, and they are the direct precursors of the musical form *romance corrido* (*corrido* for short). It is possible to trace the changing historical consciousness of the Hispano people in the New World by examining the evolution of their narrative ballads and the shift from the *romance* to the *corrido*.

Without humor, despair could prevail. While much of the vocal music of the Hispano Southwest emphasizes episodes that depict the harshness of existence of a passionate people in what at times must have seemed an indifferent landscape, there are certain songs that could only have emanated from the funny bone of *la gente*. Some of these songs are included within the musical form known as the *relación*. This form is similar to both the *romance* and the *corrido* in that it assumes a narrative form. The distinguished Mexican ethnomusicologist Vicente T. Mendoza includes the *relaciones* with the children's game songs, or *juegos infantiles*. They are frequently humorous and assume absurd proportions. As John D. Robb has pointed out, Mendoza includes *disparates, relaciones aglutinantes, mentiras,* and others under the heading of *relaciones*. Robb has simplified matters by stating that the term itself is applied in Mexico "to a type of humorous folk song characterized by lists of things, people or places." He continues by indicating that the *disparate* deals with exaggeration and that the *mentiras* are tall stories. Rubén Cobos defines the *relación* as "a type of folk song dealing with some absurdity as a theme and narrating exploits of animals or insects in an exaggerated manner." By these definitions the *romances Don Gato* and *La trejaria del piojo y la liendre* could also be regarded as *relaciones*, even though they are considered *romances* by Aurelio Espinosa and Arthur Campa.

Vicente T. Mendoza made outstanding contributions to the body of knowledge that pertains to Mexican traditional music; his thorough research and subsequent publications comprise much of our understanding of that subject. Mendoza indicates that the *relación* as a form extends back nearly five centuries into antiquity, to the time of Juan del Encina, who was one of the foremost Spanish composers of narrative ballads and other musical forms. Gilbert Chase regarded del Encina as "the foremost of the poet musicians who flourished during the time of Ferdinand and Isabel" (1468–1529), a critical time for the New World.

It is fascinating to discover permutations of folk songs that have endured for centuries within cultural enclaves in relative isolation from each other. In the encyclopedic collection of folk music assembled by Mendoza are folk songs that are still recollected in Hispano settlements of the northern reaches of New Mexico and southern Colorado. Some of these songs are considered to be of Spanish provenance or at least to have counterparts in Spain.

Romances and *relaciones* such as *Delgadina, Mambrú se fue a la guerra, Don Gato, La rana,* and *La trejaria del piojo y la liendre* are still to be found north of the border, all of which are included by Mendoza in his book *Lírica infantil de México*, published in 1951.

Probably the best known of the *romances* of yore is *Delgadina*, classified by Aurelio Espinosa as a novelesque ballad and regarded by Arthur Campa and Enrique R. Lamadrid as ubiquitous in the Spanish-speaking world. In 1946 Campa listed sources of no less than fifty-four different versions of this *romance*, which recounts the dire deeds of a king who lusted after his daughter. When she refused to comply with his licentious demands, he cruelly allowed her to die of thirst and hunger.

This version of *Delgadina* was performed by Crescencio M. García, who was born in Mimbres, New Mexico, in 1916. Señor García learned this version from his mother, who used to sing to him when he was a boy. This version differs textually and melodically from any of those presented by Mendoza, although in both lyrics and melody it is recognizably the same song. It is also melodically similar to a version recorded in Arizona in 1947, which appears in John D. Robb's great work. Robb included eleven versions of *Delgadina*, four of which are still known in Spain.

One of the versions cited by Mendoza has an *estribillo,* or refrain, that onomatopoeically sounds the toll of the bell. Enrique R. Lamadrid has noted that the final verse of Crescencio García's *Delgadina* exemplifies a poetic convention dating from medieval times, where the troubadour singing beneath a tree is a favorite image of the *despedida,* or farewell verses, of a ballad.

Delgadina

Crescencio M. García

Delgadina se paseaba
en su sala muy cuadrada,
con su manto de hilo de oro
que en su pecho iluminaba.

"Levántate, Delgadina,
ponte tu falda de seda,
porque nos vamos a misa
a la ciudad de Morelia."

Cuando salieron de misa
su papá le platicaba,
"Delgadina, hija mía,
yo te quiero para dama."

"No lo quiera Dios, papá,
ni la Virgen Soberana.
Es ofensa para Dios
y traición para mi mama."

"Luego que lleguemos a casa
yo te pondré en castigo
por hija desobediente
no a vedar lo que te digo."

"Júntense los once criados,"
dice el padre de Delgadina.
"Enciérrenla en un cuarto oscuro
donde la voz sea ladina.

Si le dieren que comer
la comida muy salada
si le dieren que tomar
la del agua sorrostrada."

"Madrecita de mi vida,
tu castigo estoy sufriendo.
Regálame un vaso de agua
que de sed me estoy muriendo."

"Júntense los once criados,"
dice la madre de Delgadina.
"Llévenle agua a Delgadina
en esos vasitos de oro,
sobre bordados de China."

Delgadina

Crescencio M. García

Delgadina was strolling
in her well-squared hall,
with her mantle of golden threads
that illuminated her breast.

"Arise, Delgadina,
put on your silken dress,
because we are going to mass
in the city of Morelia."

When they left mass,
her father said,
"Delgadina, my daughter,
I want you as my mistress."

"God would not wish that, father,
nor the Sovereign Virgen.
It is an offense against God
and treachery against my mother."

"After we get home
I will start your punishment
for being a disobedient daughter
who should not deny what I ask."

"Bring forth my eleven servants,"
says Delgadina's father.
"Confine her in a dark room
where her voice will sound foreign.

If you feed her
give her very salty food,
and if you give her drink,
throw water in her face."

"My dearest mother,
I am suffering your punishment.
Give me a glass of water
for I am dying of thirst."

"Bring forth my eleven servants,"
says Delgadina's mother.
"Take water to Delgadina
in these golden glasses,
on Chinese embroidery."

Cuando le llevaron el agua,
Delgadina estaba muerta,
como gallo, boca arriba,
tenía su boquita abierta.

La cama de Delgadina
de ángeles está coronada,
y la de su papá el rey
de demonios apretada.

Ya con esta me despido
por las azahares de lima,
aquí se acaba cantando
la obediente Delgadina.

When they took her the water,
Delgadina was dead,
like a rooster face up,
with her little mouth open.

Delgadina's bed
with angels was crowned,
while that of her father the king
was crowded with demons.

With this I take my leave
by the blossoms of a lime tree,
here I cease singing
of the obedient Delgadina.

Delgadina

Performed by Crescencio M. García

Another type of *romance* addressed by Aurelio Espinosa is the burlesque ballad, in which the hero is not necessarily distinguished and may even be other than human. These *romances* are regarded as burlesque because of their droll comedy. *Don Gato* tells the tale of a cat whose amorous pursuits lead to a fatal end. Versions of this ballad have been noted in New Mexico, Texas, Mexico, Chile, Argentina, Cuba, Santo Domingo, and Puerto Rico, indicating that it has enjoyed wide popularity. It is thought by some to have originated in Portugal and by others in Spain. It has many permutations, and the texts of the known versions are highly diversified. In one version noted by Arthur Campa, the attending physician, Don Carlos, was reputed to be a well-known physician along the Mexican border. A physician named Ventura Lobato, mentioned in the ballad presented here, actually practiced in the vicinity of Tomé, New Mexico, in the nineteenth century. In other versions of this *romance*, the names of other doctors appear. In a version noted by Robb, Don Gato was chasing a beautiful Moorish pussy at the time of his accident.

This version of *Don Gato* was sung by Edwin Berry, the master folk singer from Tomé, New Mexico. Señor Berry has committed many hundreds of folk songs to memory and may be regarded as one of the greatest loremasters of his time. At one time Señor Berry suffered from blindness and enlisted the aid of *el Médico Divino* by singing *penitente alabados,* or hymns of praise. After four months he regained his eyesight and fulfilled the promise of reestablishing the *penitente morada,* or chapel, in Adelino, New Mexico.

In 1983 Señor Berry was filmed performing *Don Gato* for the documentary film *La Música de los Viejos.*

Don Gato

Edwin Berry

Estaba el señor Don Gato
sentado en su silla de oro
gastando medias de seda
y zapatos colorados.

Cuando llega su compadre
le propone si quería ser casado
con una gata morena
que andaba sobre el tejado.

Y Don Gato por verla pronto
brincó de costilla abajo
y se quebró una costilla
y se desconsartó un brazo.

Miau, miau, miau …

Mandaron por el doctor,
Don Ventura Lobato
y a las cuatro de la mañana
ya era difunto el gato.

Sir Cat

Edwin Berry

Don Gato, the cat
was sitting on his golden chair
wearing his silk stockings
and crimson shoes.

When his friend arrives
he asks if he would like to marry
a dark moorish cat
who was walking on the roof.

Don Gato, in his haste to see her
leapt and fell on his side
and broke a rib
and dislocated his arm.

Meow, meow, meow …

They sent for the doctor,
Don Ventura Lobato,
but by four in the morning
the cat was already dead.

Los ratones de alegría
se visten de colorado
y los gatitos chiquitos
se quedan desconsolados.

Miau, miau, miau, miau.

The mice, overcome with joy,
dressed up in crimson
but the little kittens
could not be consoled.

Meow, meow, meow, meow, meow.

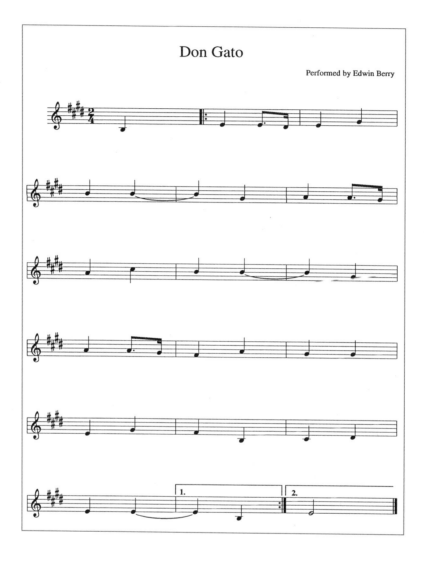

Don Gato

Performed by Edwin Berry

Note: All transcriptions of Spanish lyrics are verbatim and are based
on actual performances. The unique flavor of New Mexican Spanish
derives from its seventeenth-century archaisms and playful colloquial-
isms. Occasionally, singers will also transpose or change words of
familiar songs. ¡Que viva la música!

The Spanish language lends itself beautifully to assonance and rhyme. The following tongue twister illustrates the use of nonsense syllables in the speech play that is such a necessary part of the linguistic development of children. It was playfully recited by Solomón Chávez in Alamosa, Colorado.

Trabalenguas

Solomón Chávez

¡Estaba una madre,
godable, piricotable, tarantantable,
que tenía tres hijos,
godijos, piricotijos, tarantantijos.

Esta madre,
godable, piricotable, tarantantable,
les dijo a sus hijos,
godijos, piricotijos, tarantantijos,
"Ir al monte,
gondonte, piricontonte, tarantantonte,
y tráeme un liebre,"
godiebre, piricotiebre, tarantantiebre.

Fueron los hijos,
godijos, piricotijos, tarantantijos,
al monte,
godonte, piricontonte, tarantantonte,
y le trujieron una liebre,
godiebre, piricotiebre, tarantantiebre,
a su madre
godabre, piricotable, tarantantable.

La pusieron en la mesa,
godesa, piricotesa, tarantantesa,
y vido un gato,
godaso, piricotaso, tarantantaso,
y se comió el liebre,
godiebre, piricotiebre, tarantantiebre,
que los hijos,
godijos, piricotijos, tarantantijos,
habían traído a su madre,
godable, piricotable, tarantantable!

Tongue Twister

Solomón Chávez

There was a mother,
godother, piricotother, tarantantother,
who had three sons,
godons, piricotons, tarantantons.

This mother,
godother, piricotother, tarantantother,
said to her sons,
godons, piricotons, tarantantons,
"Go to the mountain,
godountain, piricotountain, tarantantountain,
and fetch me a hare,"
godare, piricotare, tarantantare.

The three sons went,
godent, prircotent, tarantantent,
to the mountain,
godountain, piricotountain, tarantantountain,
and brought back a hare,
godare, piricotare, tarantantare,
to their mother,
godother, piricotother, tarantantother.

They put it on the table,
godable, piricotable, tarantantable,
and a cat saw,
godaw, piricotaw, tarantantaw,
and ate the hare,
godare, piricotare, tarantantare,
that the three sons,
godons, piricotons, tarantantons,
had brought to their mother,
godother, piricotother, tarantantother!

Another of the burlesque *romances* is *La trejaria del piojo y la liendre*, the wedding feast of the louse and the nit. This very old song is known in both New Mexico and Mexico, and at least two counterparts have been noted in Spain. This version was performed by Abade Martínez, who has spent most of his lifetime in the town of San Luis, Colorado. His repertoire includes several songs of great antiquity that reflect the extraordinary longevity of the oral tradition of Hispano culture in the Río Grande del Norte. Señor Martínez's performance of this humorous old ballad is extremely well executed and elicits a sense of how this music has sounded for centuries.

La trejaria del piojo y la liendre

Abade Martínez

El piojo y la liendre se iban a casar,
y no se casaron por falta de pan.

estribillo:
Tirla, dirla, dirla, da,
tirla, dirla, dirla, da.

Responde una vaca desde su corral,
"Síganse las bodas que yo pondré el pan."

estribillo

Síganse las bodas que si ya pan tenemos,
ahora dinero, ¿dónde hallaremos?

estribillo

Responde un becerro desde su chiquero,
"Síganse las bodas, yo pondré el dinero."

estribillo

Síganse las bodas, dinero tenemos,
ahora la carne, ¿dónde la hallaremos?

estribillo

Responde un coyote, galgo muerto de hambre,
"Síganse las bodas, yo pondré la carne."

estribillo

Síganse las bodas, ya carne tenemos,
ahora cocinera, ¿dónde hallaremos?

estribillo

Responde una chinche desde su chinchal,
"Síganse las bodas, yo iré a cocinar."

estribillo

The Wedding of the Louse and the Nit

Abade Martínez

The louse and the nit were going to be wed,
but marry they couldn't, because there was no bread.
chorus:
Dee-da-la, dee-da-la, dee-da-la, da
dee-da-la, dee-da-la, dee-da-la, dum.

A cow calls out from her corral,
"Carry on with the wedding, I'll give the bread."

chorus

On with the wedding, since we have bread,
but now, where will we find money?

chorus

A calf calls out from his stall,
"Carry on with the wedding, I'll give the money."

chorus

On with the wedding, since we have money,
now what about meat, where will we find some?

chorus

A skinny coyote answers, starving to death,
"Carry on with the wedding, I'll give the meat."

chorus

On with the wedding, now we have meat,
but where can we find a cook?

chorus

A bed bug calls out from her bed bug house,
"Carry on with the wedding, I'll be the cook."

chorus

Síganse las bodas, cocinera tenemos,
ahora padrinos, ¿dónde hallaremos?

estribillo

Responde un ratón de su ratonal,
"Amarren los gatos y yo iré a padrinear."

estribillo

Síganse las bodas, padrino tenemos
ahora madrina, ¿dónde hallaremos?

estribillo

Responde una araña desde su arañal
"Síganse las bodas, yo iré a madrinear."

estribillo

Síganse las bodas, padrinos tenemos,
ahora quién toca, ¿dónde hallaremos?

estribillo

Responde un grillo desde su grillal,
"Síganse las bodas, yo iré a tocar."

estribillo

Síganse las bodas, que el toque tenemos,
ahora quién baile, ¿dónde hallaremos?

estribillo

Fuimos hasta Africa a traer bailadores,
responden los changos, "Ahí vamos, señores."

estribillo

En la primera mesa repartiendo el vino,
suéltanse los gatos, sóplanse al padrino.

estribillo

Se acaba la bulla, se acaba el fandango,
al pobre padrino lo llevan mascando.

estribillo

En la madrugada que el gallo cantó,
no hubo ni un chango que no se trompeó.

estribillo

Salen los perros haciendo algarazo,
salen los piojos tirando balazos.

estribillo

On with the wedding, we have a cook,
now what about godparents, where can we find
    some?

chorus

A rat answers from his rat's nest,
"Tie up the cats and I'll do the godfathering."

chorus

On with the wedding, we have a godfather,
now where can we find a godmother?

chorus

A spider answers from her spidery realm,
"Carry on with the wedding, I'll do the godmothering."

chorus

On with the wedding, since we have godparents,
now who will play music, and where can we find
    them?

chorus

A cricket calls out from his cricket hole,
"Carry on with the wedding, I'll make the music."

chorus

On with the wedding, we have the music,
now who will dance and where can we find them?

chorus

We went clear to Africa to bring back dancers,
"Here we come, señores," say the monkeys.

chorus

At the head table, the wine is flowing,
the cats get loose, swallow the godfather.

chorus

The excitement is over, the fandango is finished,
and the poor godfather, they chewed him up.

chorus

Early in the morning, when the cock crowed,
there was not one monkey that didn't get punched.

chorus

The dogs come out with their battle cries,
the lice come out shooting their guns.

chorus

La trejaria del piojo y la liendre

Performed by Abade Martínez

In part oral tradition acts as a vehicle for transmitting the ethos of a culture through the generations, passed down through the collective memory of a culture. It is a body of remembered parts. The success of each part is contingent upon its relevance and the energy it commands within the whole.

Within Anglo tradition the children's game song *Ring around the Rosey* alludes to the Black Death, the bubonic and pneumonic plague, which in the fourteenth century claimed as many as twenty-five million human lives in Europe. This song has prevailed for six centuries, although its origins have faded from collective recollection. Time has an effect on the way history is perceived. In some instances the communal memory of a given event goes through a process of transmogrification and assumes a form that is incorporated into children's play. An elder frequently has greater ease in recalling a song learned in childhood than one learned in adulthood. An octogenarian recalled a whole series of songs that he claimed to have learned at the age of five years; however, he was unable to recall a single song learned thereafter. The staying power of children's songs is formidable.

The Spanish *romances* of yore deal with events that have long since ceased to be relevant to the Hispanos of the New World. The reckless military adventures of the English Duke of Marlborough, dead now for over two and a half centuries, are recalled in the *romance Mambrú se fue a la guerra,* which is included in the *Lírica infantil de México* and remains as part of the tradition of the Río Grande del Norte. *Mambrú* is a corruption of the name *Marlborough,* and the song is descended from a historic event that was long since forgotten except by students of history. Imagine the surprise of the Duke of Marlborough, John Churchill, a distant ancestor of Winston Churchill, if he only knew that his memory is still sustained in this fashion. The version presented here was sung by Edwin Berry of Tomé, New Mexico.

## *Mambrú se fue a la guerra*	## Mambrú Went to War
Edwin Berry	Edwin Berry

Mambrú se fue a la guerra
¿no sé cuándo vendrá,
si vendrá por la Pascua
o por la Navidad,
o por la Navidad
o por la Navidad?

Ya veo venir un paje,
miren, ¡Dominus! ustedes,
¡qué salvaje!
Ya veo venir un paje,
¿qué noticia traerá,
qué noticia traerá,
qué noticia traerá?

La noticia que traigo,
miren, ¡Dominus! ustedes,
¡que me caigo!
La noticia que traigo,
Mambrú se ha muerto ya,
Mambrú se ha muerto ya,
Mambrú se ha muerto ya.

Debajo de un sabino,
miren, ¡Dominus! ustedes,
¡que me empino!
Debajo de un sabino,
lo van a sepultar,
lo van a sepultar
lo van a sepultar.

Los padres malancota,
miren, ¡Dominus! ustedes,
¡qué pelota!
Los padres malancota
lo van a sepultar,
lo van a sepultar,
lo van a sepultar.

Mambrú went to war,
I know not when he will return,
if he will come for Easter,
or for Christmas,
or for Christmas,
or for Christmas?

Already I see a page coming.
Lord! Look you,
What a savage!
Already I see a page coming,
what message does he bring,
what message does he bring,
what message does he bring?

The message that I bring
Lord! Look you,
how I fall!
The message that I bring
is that Mambrú has already died,
is that Mambrú has already died,
is that Mambrú has already died.

Underneath a cedar,
Lord! Look you,
how drunk I am!
Underneath a cedar
they will bury him,
they will bury him,
they will bury him.

The Malancot fathers,
Lord! Look you,
what a naked shame!
The Malancot fathers,
are going to bury him,
are going to bury him,
are going to bury him.

Mambrú se fue a la guerra

Performed by Edwin Berry

Los Diez Mandamientos

Performed by Anita y Albino Gómez, y Cipriano Vigil

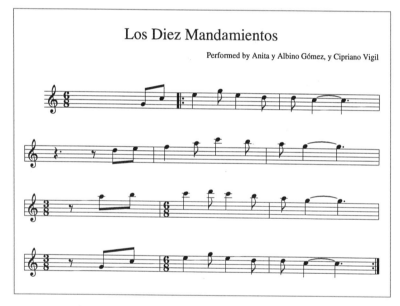

Religious songs also have a proclivity for long life. The profound subjectivity common to both children's songs and religious songs is also inherent in the mythic structure of a culture. Human involvement on a collective level is extremely complex when experienced within a cultural mythos. Therein lies a sense of continuity, relevance, and personal and collective meaning. Tradition finds expression in music, both secular and sacred, and helps to maintain the alignment of the mythic coordinates of a culture. When music is performed, a chord of recognition is struck and a sense of mutual recollection or collective memory is evoked. This process is integrated into the ceremonial reenactment of myths.

A burlesque *romance* that integrates both religious elements and some sense of parody is *Los Diez Mandamientos,* or the *Ten Commandments.* Arthur Campa mentions "the tendency among Hispano people to parody in a harmless way, various passages from the Bible." Here the singer confesses she has broken almost all the commandments for the sake of love. This version was sung by Anita Gómez, accompanied by Cipriano Vigil and her husband, Albino, at the Gómez home in Las Tablas, New Mexico. It resembles the New Mexican version Campa included in his publication of 1946. Campa did not include a melodic transcription, however.

Los Diez Mandamientos	**The Ten Commandments**
Anita & Albino Gómez	Anita & Albino Gómez

Oye, encanto de mi vida
alegría de mis tormentos,
sólo porque he quebrantado
de Dios los Diez Mandamientos.

El primero amar a Dios.
Yo no lo amo como debo,
sólo por pensar en ti,
hermosísimo lucero.

El segundo es no jurar.
Yo mil veces he jurado,
de no comer ni beber
hasta no verme a tu lado.

El tercero es oír misa.
No la oigo con devoción,
sólo por pensar en ti,
dueña de mi corazón.

El cuarto honor a mis padres.
La obediencia les perdí,
en público y en secreto,
sólo por amarte a ti.

Listen, darling of my life,
joy of my torments,
only because I have broken
God's Ten Commandments.

The first is to love God.
I don't love him as I should,
only because I think of you,
my most beautiful star.

The second is not to swear.
A thousand times I have sworn,
to not eat or drink
until I am by your side.

The third is to hear mass.
I don't listen with devotion,
only because I think of you,
lady of my heart.

The fourth is to honor my parents.
I have lost obedience to them,
in public and in secret,
just for loving you.

El quinto es no matar.
Este sí no he quebrantado,
pero mataré el alevoso,
al que yo encuentre a tu lado.

Yo del sexto no me acuso,
no me debo de acusar,
porque me da pensamiento
he sabido yo pecar.

El séptimo es no robar,
la venia no es permitido,
robaré esas tres coronas,
para ti, bien de mi vida.

El octavo es no levantar
ningún falso testimonio,
de eso no me acuso yo,
ahí se acusa el demonio.

El noveno es no desear
la mujer de otro marido.
Porque cierto lo deseas
pronto te echará al olvido.

Ya que son Diez Mandamientos,
sólo se encierran en dos,
en servirte y en amarte
y en vivir juntos los dos.

The fifth is not to kill.
This one I have not broken,
but I will kill any traitor,
that I should find at your side.

Of the sixth I don't accuse myself
I shouldn't accuse myself,
because it gives me the thought,
that I have known how to sin. [commit adultery]

The seventh is not to steal,
pardons are not permitted,
I will steal those three crowns,
for you, treasure of my life.

The eighth is not to raise
false testimony against anyone,
of that one I don't accuse myself,
there the devil must be accused.

The ninth is not to desire
the wife of another man.
If it is certain you desire it,
she will quickly forget you.

Even though there are Ten Commandments,
they can be contained in two,
to serve you and to love you
and to both live together.

A *relación* that has tickled the fancy of *la gente* in the Río Grande del Norte is entitled *Frijolitos pintos*. It is a *disparate*, which is to say that it is nonsensical and comical. To the skipping rhythm of the *chotís*, or schottische, the impossible pain of love is compared to a spotted dog chasing its tail. It has an *estribillo*, or refrain. The version below was performed by Toney Sánchez in the home of the late Reymundo Anaya in Clayton, New Mexico, who can be heard laughing in the background. At the time of recording, Señor Sánchez was sixty-eight years old and Señor Anaya was eighty-five.

Frijolitos pintos

Reymundo Anaya & Toney Sánchez

Frijolitos pintos,
claveles morados,
¡Ay, cómo sufren
los enamorados!

Mamacita linda,
allí viene Vicente,
sácale un banquito
para que se siente.

Le dio la viruela,
le dio el sarampión,
le quedó la cara
como un chicharrón.

Mamacita linda,
allí viene Vicente,
sácale un banquito
para que se siente.

Una perra pinta,
pinta y orejona,
se buscó la cola
y la tenía rabona.

Mamacita linda,
allí viene Vicente,
sácale un banquito
para que se siente.

Little Pinto Beans

Reymundo Anaya & Toney Sánchez

Little pinto beans,
purple carnations,
Oh, how they suffer,
those who are in love!

Pretty little mama,
here comes Vicente,
pull him out a bench
so he can sit down.

He caught chickenpox,
he caught measles,
his face was left
like a fried pigskin.

Pretty little mama,
here comes Vicente,
pull him out a bench
so he can sit down.

A spotted dog,
spotted and big-eared,
was looking for her tail,
but found it was bobbed.

Pretty little mama,
here comes Vicente,
pull him out a bench
so he can sit down.

Frijolitos pintos

Performed by Toney Sánchez con Reymundo Anaya

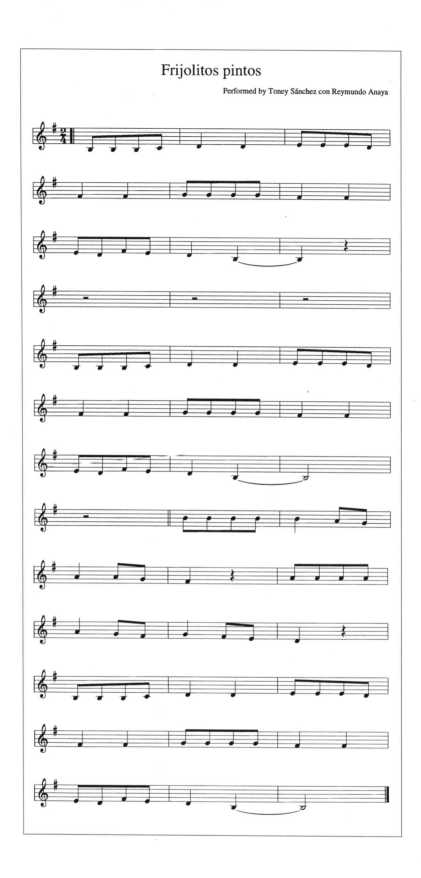

Enrique Yara was born in 1892 and spent much of his long life in Watrous, New Mexico. Even though he was all but blind, he chose to live alone in his adobe home, with his dog for a companion. He played both the guitar and the mandolin. When we recorded him in 1978, he claimed to recall few songs that he had learned after the age of five years. Presented here is his rendition of *Corre, corre caballito*. Vicente Mendoza includes fragments of a song entitled *Corre, caballo* that is similar to the version performed by Enrique Yara. It dates from 1831 and probably originated in San Luis Potosí, Mexico.

Corre, corre, caballito	**Run, Run, Little Pony**
Enrique Yara	Enrique Yara

Corre, corre, caballito,	Run, run, little pony,
corre, corre alrededor,	run, run around,
con la línea los monteros	all in line, the hunters,
que no dejen de jugar.	may they never stop their game.
Veinte pesos va la chota	Twenty pesos on the calf
y al caballo se lo juego, :1	and I'll play you the pony, :1
y a la chota por bolita	and the calf scuffles,
y al caballo por ligero.	but the pony is faster.
repite 1	*repeat 1*
Corre, corre, caballito,	Run, run, little pony,
corre, corre sin cesar. :2	run, run without ceasing, :2
Anda, alínea los monteros,	go on, line up the hunters,
que no dejen de jugar.	may they never stop their game.
repite 2	*repeat 2*
repite 1	*repeat 1*
repite 2	*repeat 2*

Corre, corre caballito

Performed by Enrique Yara

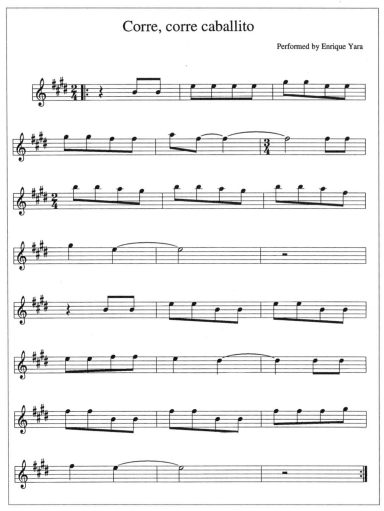

La rana

Performed by Solomón Chávez

A *relación aglutinante* is a form of ballad wherein each verse contains an ever-growing list of subjects attached or "stuck" to the song. In the Velásquez *Diccionario de los idiomas inglés y español, aglutinante* is defined as sticking plaster. Indeed, the word "glue" may be perceived therein. An English example of the use of the *aglutinante* is *The Twelve Days of Christmas.* The example presented here is entitled *La rana*. It was performed by Señor Solomón Chávez of Alamosa, Colorado, who was distinguished for his knowledge of Hispano culture, folk music, and folklore. *La rana* is an excellent example of the *relación aglutinante*, a form regarded by many as a playful mnemonic exercise for children.

La rana

Solomón Chávez

Estaba cantando la rana
debajo del agua.

Cuando la rana salió a cantar,
vino la mosca y le hizo callar.
La mosca a la rana,
la rana que estaba cantando, sentada
debajo del agua.

Cuando la mosca salió a cantar,
vino la araña y le hizo callar.
La araña a la mosca,
la mosca a la rana,
la rana que estaba sentada, cantando
debajo del agua.

Cuando la araña salió a cantar,
vino la escoba y le hizo callar.
La escoba a la araña,
la araña a la mosca,
la mosca a la rana,
la rana que estaba sentada, cantando
debajo del agua.

Cuando la escoba salió a cantar,
vino el ratón y le hizo callar.
El ratón a la escoba,
la escoba a la araña,
la araña a la mosca,
la mosca a la rana,
la rana que estaba sentada, cantando
debajo del agua.

The Frog

Solomón Chávez

The frog was singing
under the water.

When the frog came out to sing,
along came the fly and made him be quiet.
The fly hushed the frog,
the frog that was singing, sitting
under the water.

When the fly came out to sing,
along came the spider and made him be quiet.
The spider hushed the fly,
the fly hushed the frog,
the frog that was sitting, singing
under the water.

When the spider came out to sing,
along came the broom and made her be quiet.
The broom hushed the spider,
the spider hushed the fly,
the fly hushed the frog,
the frog that was sitting, singing
under the water.

When the broom came out to sing,
along came the mouse and made her be quiet.
The mouse hushed the broom,
the broom hushed the spider,
the spider hushed the fly,
the fly hushed the frog,
the frog that was sitting, singing
under the water.

Cuando el ratón salió a cantar,
vino el gato y le hizo callar.
El gato al ratón,
el ratón a la escoba,
la escoba a la araña,
la araña a la mosca,
la mosca a la rana,
la rana que estaba sentada, cantando
debajo del agua.

Cuando el gato salió a cantar,
vino el perro y le hizo callar.
El perro al gato,
el gato al ratón,
el ratón a la escoba,
la escoba a la araña,
la araña a la mosca,
la mosca a la rana,
la rana que estaba sentada, cantando
debajo del agua.

Cuando el perro salió a cantar,
vino el hombre y le hizo callar.
El hombre al perro,
el perro al gato,
el gato al ratón,
el ratón a la escoba,
la escoba a la araña,
la araña a la mosca,
la mosca a la rana,
la rana que estaba sentada, cantando
debajo del agua.

Cuando el hombre salió a cantar,
vino la suegra y le hizo
    callar.
La suegra al hombre,
el hombre al perro,
el perro al gato,
el gato al ratón,
el ratón a la escoba,
la escoba a la araña,
la araña a la mosca,
la mosca a la rana,
la rana que estaba sentada, cantando
debajo del agua.

Cuando la suegra salió a cantar,
¡ni el mismo Diablo le hizo
    callar!

When the mouse came out to sing,
along came the cat and made him be quiet.
The cat hushed the mouse,
the mouse hushed the broom,
the broom hushed the spider,
the spider hushed the fly,
the fly hushed the frog,
the frog that was sitting, singing
under the water.

When the cat came out to sing,
along came the dog and made her be quiet.
The dog hushed the cat,
the cat hushed the mouse,
the mouse hushed the broom,
the broom hushed the spider,
the spider hushed the fly,
the fly hushed the frog,
the frog that was sitting, singing
under the water.

When the dog came out to sing,
along came the man and made him be quiet.
The man hushed the dog,
the dog hushed the cat,
the cat hushed the mouse,
the mouse hushed the broom,
the broom hushed the spider,
the spider hushed the fly,
the fly hushed the frog,
the frog that was sitting, singing
under the water.

When the man came out to sing,
along came his mother-in-law and made him be
    quiet.
The mother-in-law hushed the man,
the man hushed the dog,
the dog hushed the cat,
the cat hushed the mouse,
the mouse hushed the broom,
the broom hushed the spider,
the spider hushed the fly,
the fly hushed the frog,
the frog that was sitting, singing
under the water.

When the mother-in-law came out to sing,
not even the Devil himself could make her be
    quiet!

The most popular *relación* still performed in New Mexico is *Mi carrito paseado*. The first Model T Fords rolled into New Mexico with repair manuals written in English. With few translations, names for car parts were adapted directly into Spanish. Terms like *"cranque"* and *"esparque"* still provoke laughter and the comic vision of a broken down jalopy. This *relación* was composed in the late 1920s by Severo Mondragón of Antón Chico, New Mexico. Robb includes a printed version of this song in his 1954 publication "Hispanic Folk Songs of New Mexico." The melody line of Robb's version differs slightly from the version included here, which was recorded in 1987 and was performed by Roberto Mondragón, son of the composer.

Roberto Mondragón is very well known throughout the region as a former New Mexico lieutenant governor, folk musician, and radio personality. He has been instrumental in reviving interest in *Nuevo Mexicano* culture through the region of the Río Grande del Norte.

Mi carrito paseado

Tengo un carro muy paseado
que el que no lo ha experimentado
no lo puede hacer rodar.

No más tomo yo el asiento
y se levanta como el viento
casi lo hago hasta volar.

Tiene los fenders ladeados
y los tires bien gastados
tiene techo de cartón.

Tiene roto el radiator,
descompuesto el generator,
se quebró la transmisión.

No tiene ni batería,
se la quité el otro día,
porque estaba hasta al revés.

Y aunque el starter se atranque
le echo agua y le doy cranque
y aquí voy volando en tres.

El otro día allá en la mesa
se me puso en la cabeza
de salir a andar por allí.

Le eché agua a mi cucaracha
prendí un fósforo a mi vacha
y salí volando en high.

My Jalopy

I have a car so totally beat
whoever has never driven it
will never get it rolling.

I just get in the seat
and it takes off like the wind
and I almost make it fly.

The fenders are crooked
the tires are worn out
the roof is of cardboard.

The radiator is leaking.
the generator is shot,
the transmission is broken.

It doesn't even have a battery
I took it out the other day
because it was in backwards.

Though the starter is stuck
I put in water and crank it
and go flying off in third.

The other day on the mesa
I got it in my head
to go for a drive out there.

I put water in my cockroach,
lit a match to my cigarette butt,
and went off flying in high.

Llegué derecho al Atarque,
le bajé todo el esparque,
y al llegar se me murió.

Le buscaba yo a aquel carro,
no le hallaba más que sarro
entre las bandas de low.

Y a un hombre que allí pasaba
lo llamé pa' donde estaba
y le di mi parecer.

Yo le doy este espantajo
pa' que lo tire al carajo
donde no lo vuelva a ver.

I went straight to Atarque,
lowered all the spark,
and it died when we arrived.

I looked for that car and
found it was all crudded up
between the low and drive.

Then a man passed by
I called him over
and told him what I thought.

I'll give you this wreck
so you can get rid of it
where I'll never see it again.

Mi carrito paseado

Performed by Roberto Mondragón

For centuries after the Spanish conquest, the Hispanos of northern New Mexico lived in isolated villages and maintained only the most meager contact with their more cosmopolitan neighbors many hundreds of miles to the south. The winters were deep with snow and frozen into inactivity, a time of reflection and renewal.

The need for diversion overcame the inertia of the season, and the playing of games became a social pastime in which the participants delighted. One such game is called *el cañute* (the reed or pipe). This game involved the use of four hollow reeds about eight inches in length, which were assigned different values and which were distinguished by their hues or the marks carved on them. Each was given a name: *el uno, el dos, el mulato* and *el cinchado* (one, two, dark one, and one with a string around it). *El mulato* was worth four points, *el cinchado* three points, *el dos* two, and *el uno* only one point. Each team had the same number of players. The team in current possession of *los cañutes* hid beneath a blanket in their corner of the room and inserted a slender stick or nail into one of the *cañutes,* then buried all four of the *cañutes* in a pile of sand. They then emerged from beneath the blanket and signaled the opposing team to come over and guess in which *cañute* the stick had been placed. There were variations as to how the game was played, and sometimes the stakes were high. Versions of this native betting game are known to have been played by various Indian cultures. For example the Yuman Indians played a guessing game that employed shafts placed in the leg bone of a white crane. In several New Mexico pueblos, a similar game is played throughout the night in front of the church on the eve of the Day of the Dead (November 2).

This version of *Los cañuteros* was performed by Señor Abade Martínez in San Luis, Colorado. It has characteristics of the musical form known as the *indita* and evokes a strong sense of a former time in the history of the bioregion of the Río Grande del Norte.

### *Los cañuteros*	### The Reed Game Players
Abade Martínez	Abade Martínez

Allí vienen los cañuteros,	There come the cañuteros,
los que vienen por el mío,	those that come for mine,
pero de allá que llevarán	but from there they'll take
rasguidos en el fondillo.	scratches on their behinds.
estribillo:	*chorus:*
Hállalo, hállalo,	*Look for it, look for it,*
cañutero sí, cañutero no,	*cañutero yes, cañutero no,*
el palito andando.	*little stick goes around.*
Parece que viene gente	Looks like people are coming,
hay rastros en la cañada,	there are signs up in the canyon,
parece que se lo llevan	looks like they have it with them,
pero no se llevan nada.	but they don't have anything.
estribillo	*chorus*
Padre mío, San Antonio,	San Antonio, my father,
devoto de los morenos,	revered by the dark-skinned,

es verdad que alzamos trigo,
pero todo lo debemos.

estribillo

En el año de la nevada
me enamoré de una tetona
En una teta me acostaba,
con la otra me cobijaba.
De lo a gusto que dormía
hasta en la cama me meaba.

(risa)

cañutero sí, cañutero no,
el palito andando.

it is true we raise wheat,
but we owe everything.

chorus

In the year of the big snow,
I fell in love with a large breasted woman.
I lay down on one breast,
and covered myself with the other.
I slept so well
I even wet the bed.

(laughter)

cañutero yes, cañutero no,
little stick goes around.

Los cañuteros

Performed by Abade Martínez

CHAPTER TWO

Inditas

O NE OF THE MUSICAL FORMS that most reflects the spirit of the bioregion of the Río Grande del Norte is the *indita,* best translated as "little Indian (song or girl)." It is a form that evolved in the New World and expresses *mestizaje,* or the mixture of Indian and Spanish. Within the context of music, the pulse of the people resonates in rhythmic accord with the land that sustains them. Although *inditas* can have sacred or even burlesque qualities, the majority are narrative ballads related to the *corridos,* whose melodic structure, according to Rubén Cobos, is imitative of Indian melodies. The rhythmic patterns often juxtapose three-beat and two-beat measures. The word *indita* usually appears in the lyrics of these ballads. The melody lines are often distinctive and not restricted to the major mode in which *corridos* are almost always sung. *Estribillos,* or refrains, are common in *inditas,* and very often they take the form of vocables, the expressive nonlexical syllables that characterize much Native North American music. Robb points out that *corridos* frequently end in feminine cadences, whereas *inditas* almost always end in masculine cadences, in which the final chord falls on an accented or strong beat in the measure. Enrique R. Lamadrid further characterizes *inditas* as usually sung in the first person and with subject matter that frequently has something to do with Indians. Robb makes the interesting comment that the melody lines of *inditas* approximate the way Indian music sounds to the Hispano ear.

The origin of this form is unclear. Adrian Treviño suggests that it may have originated with the *genízaros,* or Indians held captive by the Spanish. I think that it may be an instance of convergent evolution, that is, it appeared wherever Spanish and Indian peoples maintained contact long enough for their music to begin to meld. Whatever its origin, the *indita* may be regarded as one of the most valuable expressions of the oral history of New Mexico.

Most *indita* ballads date from the territorial period of New Mexican history, between the 1846 occupation by the U.S. Army and the 1912 admission for statehood. The *Nuevo Mexicanos* sampled the new goods and lifestyle and gradually but surely incorporated themselves into national life. Many served on the side of the Union in the Civil War. The following generations of *Nuevo Mexicanos* were also anxious to prove their loyalty to the United States and Uncle Sam, their *Tío Samuel.* In 1898 they enlisted to fight Spain in the Spanish American War. The irony that the sons of *conquistadores* were now fighting Spaniards was not lost on the people of the day. In Sabinal, a popular prayer poem was written asking San Gonzaga de Abaranda and the Virgin to stop the bloodshed. When this poem entered the oral tradition it became the "*Indita de San Luis Gonzaga*," a sacred *indita*. People make devout *promesas,* or promises, to dance for the saint in return for blessings and miracles that include everything from bringing rain to curing sickness. The Native American elements in this *indita* include sacred dancing as well as the chorus, which is chanted with vocables.

Manuel Mirabal, of San Luis, New Mexico, sings this version and recalls the desperate illness of his young son many years ago, which he believes was miraculously cured by the saint.

### Indita de San Luis Gonzaga	### Indita Ballad of Saint Aloysius Gonzaga
Manuel Mirabal	Manuel Mirabal
De mi casa he venido a pasear este lugar, denme razón de San Luis que le prometí bailar. *coro:* *Yana jeya jo,* *yana jeya jo,* *yana jeya jo.* *Yana jeya jo,* *yana jeya jo.*	From my house I have come to visit this place, tell me about Saint Aloysius I promised to dance for him. *chorus:* *Yana heya ho,* *yana heya ho,* *yana heya ho.* *Yana heya ho,* *Yana heya ho,*
En el marco de esta puerta el pie derecho pondré, denme razón de San Luis y luego le bailaré.	In this doorway I will put my right foot, tell me about Saint Aloysius and then I will dance for him.
coro	*chorus*
En el marco de esta puerta el pie derecho pondré, alaba los dulces nombres de Jesús, María y José.	In this doorway I will put my right foot, praise the sweet names of Jesus, Mary, and Joseph.
coro	*chorus*
No bailo porque tengo gusto sino porque tengo alegría, bailo porque prometí a San Luis, José y María.	I do not dance for pleasure but because I am happy, I dance because I promised St. Aloysius, Joseph, and Mary.
coro	*chorus*
San Luis Gonzaga de Amarante aparecido en un puente, esta indita te compuse cuando mi hijo andaba ausente.	St. Aloysius Gonzaga of Amarante appeared on a bridge, I composed this indita for you when my son was absent.
coro	*chorus*

San Luis Gonzaga de Amarante
aparecido en la mar,
concédeme este milagro
que te prometí bailar.

coro

Dicen que la golondrina
de un volido pasó el mar,
concédeme este milagro
que te prometí bailar.

coro

Dicen que la golondrina
de un volido pasó el mar,
de las Islas Filipinas
que acabaron de pelear.

coro

De las estrellas del cielo
tengo que bajarte dos,
para hacerte una corona
como la del Niño Dios.

coro

De las estrellas del cielo
tengo que bajarte tres,
para hacerte una corona
como la de San Andrés.

coro

Oyeme, San Luis Gonzaga
mi devoto tan sagrada,
vengo a hacerte esta visita
para bien de mis pecados.

coro

Qué bonito está San Luis
parece que nos va a hablar,
junto con el Santo Niño
cuando le van a bailar.

coro

Qué bonito está San Luis
parece un granito de oro,
junto con el Santo Niño
paraditos en el coro.

coro

Santo Niñito de Atocha
tú solito no más sabes,

St. Aloysius Gonzaga of Amarante
appeared on the ocean,
grant me this miracle
I promised to dance for you.

chorus

They say the swallow
in one flight crossed the sea,
grant me this miracle
I promised to dance for you.

chorus

They say the swallow
in one flight crossed the sea,
in the Philippine Islands
they have finished fighting.

chorus

Of the stars in the sky
I need to bring down two,
to make you a crown
like the Holy Child's.

chorus

Of the stars in the sky
I need to bring down three,
to make you a crown
like Saint Andrew's.

chorus

Hear me, Saint Aloysius Gonzaga
my devoted one so sacred,
I come to make you this visit
for the atonement of my sins.

chorus

Saint Aloysius so beautiful
looks like he will speak to us,
together with the Holy Child
when they go to dance for them.

chorus

Saint Aloysius so beautiful
he looks like a nugget of gold,
together with the Holy Child
standing up in the choir.

chorus

Holy Child of Atocha
only you know

el corazón de cada uno también todas sus necesidades.	the heart of each of us and all our needs.
coro	*chorus*
Indita, indita, indita, indita de Mogollón, también las inditas dicen San Luis de mi corazón.	Indita, indita, indita, indita of Mogollón, the Indian girls also say Saint Aloysius of my heart.
coro	*chorus*
Enfermo y convaleciendo todo lleno de esperanza, aquí me tienes San Luis a pagarte tu promesa.	Sick and convalescing all full of hope, here you have me Saint Aloysius to pay you your promise.
coro	*chorus*
Viva el sol, viva la luna y la claridad del día, y viva San Luis Gonzaga y toda su compañía.	Long live the sun and moon and the clarity of day, long live St. Aloysius Gonzaga and all his company.
coro	*chorus*
Ahinco la rodilla en tierra diciendo Jesús nos valga, la Virgen nos acompañe y el Santo Angel de mi guardia.	I kneel upon the earth saying Jesus come to our aid, may the Virgin accompany us and the Holy Guardian Angel.
coro	*chorus*
Oyeme, San Luis Gonzaga ya me voy a despedir, échame tu bendición mi voz te vuelve a decir.	Hear me, Saint Aloysius Gonzaga I will take my leave, give me your blessing my voice calls to you again.
coro	*chorus*
Recibo la bendición con gran gusto y alegría, con todo el corazón la de la Virgen María.	I receive the blessing with great joy and happiness, with all my heart, that of the Virgin Mary.
coro	*chorus*

Indita de San Luis Gonzaga

Performed by Manuel Mirabal

Ramona Sánchez was born between Las Vegas and Taos, New Mexico, in 1841. Her father was a wagon master who traveled the Santa Fe Trail, which was an important commercial transportation route from 1821 until 1880, when the Santa Fe Railroad was completed. Señor Sánchez made many perilous journeys from west to east and back again through country inhabited by Indians who frequently regarded non-Indians as interlopers and thus fair game. Señor Sánchez enjoyed the friendship of many of the most hostile of these Indians and was therefore spared when the scalps of many others in his profession became part of the accoutrements of honor of the Plains Indian warrior class. Señor Sánchez told many tales to his daughter, Ramona, about his adventures with Indians and with the great herds of buffalo that were hunted for meat.

When she was still a young woman, Ramona was taught a song entitled *Los ciboleros,* concerning the tragic death of a buffalo hunter, or *cibolero.* As the years went by, Ramona taught the song to a niece, who was born in Elizabethtown, New Mexico. Her niece, in turn, taught the song to her own daughter, Virginia Bernal, who has lived her entire life in Ratón, New Mexico. In 1943 Ramona Sánchez died, at the age of 102.

Los ciboleros is also known as *La indita de Manuel Maés.* The ballad is based on a well-known story that recounts the unfortunate death of Manuel Maés when he, his brothers, and friends were buffalo hunting near the site of the present city of Amarillo, Texas, in 1863. Fabiola Cabeza de Baca mentions the event as told by El Cuate, the man who cooked at her father's ranch near Las Vegas, New Mexico. According to El Cuate: "Manuel was riding a horse which was not yet broken for the chase. As Maés went to thrust his lance into a buffalo cow, his horse shied from another buffalo and plunged toward the animal he was about to kill. The lance slipped from Manuel's hand, turning completely around with the butt hitting against the buffalo he was aiming toward. The impact and the horse plunging toward the animal caused the lance to pierce Manuel's body. We were hunting where the city of Amarillo stands today. Manuel was buried there on the *llano,* and today his grave remains unknown and unmarked, with perhaps a wheat field growing over it." Manuel relates the story of his own passing, complaining that nobody shouted "Jesús" to him at the moment of death, a traditional religious custom.

The version of *Los ciboleros* presented here was performed by Virginia Bernal in her home in Ratón in 1978. The melody is faintly modal. The guitar accompaniment is in the key of G major. The irregularity of the meter is common to folk music.

Los ciboleros

Virginia Bernal

De los que íbanos al viaje,
mi caballo es más ligero,
pero tocó la desgracia
que se volcó en un tusero,
y en eso solté la lanza
y me pasó el cuerpo entero.

Como a las tres de la tarde,
la muerte me sentenció
en los brazos de un compadre
que ni la mano me dio,
en los brazos de un compadre
que ni la mano me dio.

Como a las tres de la tarde,
la muerte me arrebató,
en los brazos de un compadre
que ni "Jesús" me gritó,
en los brazos de un compadre
que ni "Jesús" me gritó.

Orillas de una laguna
mi cuerpo está sepultado,
como si fuera yo un traidor
mis hermanos me han dejado,
como si fuera un traidor
mis hermanos me han dejado.

Cuando esta noticia llegue
a Nuevo México entero,
todos tristes sentirán
la muerte de un caballero,
todos tristes sentirán
la muerte de un caballero.

The Buffalo Hunters

Virginia Bernal

Of all of us on the journey,
my horse was the swiftest,
but misfortune struck
when it stumbled in a prairie dog hole
and my lance loosened from my grip
and passed straight through my body.

At about three in the afternoon,
death sentenced me
in the arms of a companion
who didn't even give me his hand,
in the arms of a companion
who didn't even give me his hand.

At about three in the afternoon,
death struck me down
in the arms of a companion
who didn't even shout "Jesus help you,"
in the arms of a companion
who didn't even shout "Jesus help you."

By the shore of a lake
my body is buried,
as if I were a traitor
my brothers have abandoned me,
as if I were a traitor
my brothers have abandoned me.

When this news spreads
throughout all New Mexico,
everyone will sadly mourn
the death of a caballero,
everyone will sadly mourn
the death of a caballero.

Los ciboleros

Performed by Virginia Bernal

Una indita en su chinarca

Performed by Edulia Romero

Vicente Mendoza expressed his opinion that an *indita* thought to have originated in Xochimilco, Mexico, which made its way northward to Texas and thence to New Mexico in the first third of the last century, may well have been the ballad that linked the north to the south. It is entitled *Una indita en su chinampa* and alludes to the floating gardens once common in the great lake of the Valley of Mexico. These *chinampas*, a few of which can still be seen in Xochimilco, were constructed by Indians who built rafts, covered them with soil, and then planted on them trees, fruits, vegetables, and flowers, which they then transported by canal to the markets of Mexico City.

In 1980 Señora Edulia Romero of Alamosa, Colorado, sang this very *indita*, which she called *Una indita en su chinarca*. *China* is a common term of endearment that has its origin in a Spanish colonial caste designation, *chino*, which indicated a racial blend of African, Indian, and European blood. Today in Mexico and New Mexico, *chino* means curly-haired, one of the salient physical traits of such a mixture.

In this *indita* there is an *estribillo* that is evidently in a local Indian language. Señora Romero was concerned that this chorus not express anything bad. She said that when it used to be sung, everyone laughed when they heard it, and she concluded that if it made one laugh, it couldn't be all bad. Señora Romero was seventy-five years old at the time of recording.

Una indita en su chinarca

Edulia Romero

Una indita en su chinarca
y andaba cortando flores,
y el chiní y el indito
en cuatro orejas
le decía de sus amores.

Tata ringüé, mi mama, ¿qué?
chamácate tú, la comandé.
¿Ándale qué, ándale qué,
ándale qué, chinita?
¡No chinita, indita!

Indita mía, si tú te enojas,
indita mía, me vas a dejar.
Indita mía, ya yo vuelvo
y luego, luego,
te voy a contestar.

Te voy a contestar con amor,
te voy a contestar con amor,
indita, indita, carita,
indita de amor.

Una indita en su chinarca
y andaba cortando flores,

An Indian Maiden in Her Garden

Edulia Romero

An Indian maiden in her garden
was strolling, cutting flowers
and her Indian man
on all four ears
told her of his love.

Tata ringüé, my mama, what?
chamácate tú, la comandé.
Go on, what, go on what?
Go on, what, curly headed one?
Not curly, little Indian girl!

My *indita,* if you get angry,
my *indita,* if you will leave me,
my *indita,* I will return,
and soon, soon
I will answer you.

I will answer you with love,
I will answer you with love,
indita, indita my beloved,
indita of love.

An Indian maiden in her garden
was strolling, cutting flowers

y el indito en cuatro orejas	and her Indian man in four ears
le decía de sus amores.	told her of his love.
¿Tata ringüé, mi mama, qué?	*Tata ringüé*, my mama, what?
chamácate tú, vente pa' acá	*chamácate tú*, come over here,
hazte pa' allá, hazte pa' acá.	go over there, go over here.

*O*ne of the best known of the New Mexican *inditas* is *Indita de Cochití,* which mentions the Keresan pueblo of Cochití, located on the west bank of the Río Grande opposite the Hispano village of Peña Blanca, about twenty miles south of Santa Fe. The singer of this burlesque *indita* is demeaning an Indian maiden from Cochití. Other versions are more like a lullaby. This *indita* is sung to several different melody lines. The two that appear in Robb's collection resemble the melody line of *Indio Manuel,* which appears later in this section.

Here the *Indita de Cochití* is sung by José Domingo Romero of Las Vegas, New Mexico, who alternately plays the violin. He is accompanied by his son, Remijio, who is one of the greatest *guitarristas* in northern New Mexico. The rhythm established by Remijio is characteristic of many of the *inditas* and corresponds to an *habanera* rhythm as illustrated by Vicente Mendoza. Archaic Spanish is a typical feature of many folk lyrics in New Mexico. Here *seiga* is an archaic form of *sea* ("I may be").

Indita de Cochití	**Indian Maiden from Cochití**
José D. Romero	José D. Romero
Indita, indita, indita,	*Indita, indita, indita,*
indita de Cochití,	*indita* from Cochití,
no le hace que seiga indita	it doesn't matter that you are Indian,
si al cabo no soy pa' ti.	if in the end I'm not for you.
Indita, indita, indita,	*Indita, indita, indita,*
indita de Cochití,	*indita* from Cochití,
no le hace que seiga indita	it doesn't matter that you are Indian,
si al cabo no soy pa' ti.	if in the end I'm not for you.
Indita, indita, indita,	*Indita, indita, indita,*
indita del otro lado,	*indita* from the other side,
¿en dónde andabas anoche	where were you last night
que traes el ojo pegado?	to get that swollen eye?
Indita, indita, indita,	*Indita, indita, indita,*
indita del otro lado,	*indita* from the other side,
¿en dónde andabas anoche	where were you last night
que traes el ojo pegado?	to get that swollen eye?

Indita de Cochití

Performed by José D. y Remijio Romero

Indita, indita, indita,
indita del otro día,
¿en dónde andabas anoche
que traiga barriga fría?

Indita, indita, indita,
indita del otro día,
¿en dónde andabas anoche
.que traiga barriga fría?

Indita, indita, indita,
indita de Cochití,
no le hace que seiga indita
si al cabo no soy pa' ti.

Indita, indita, indita,
indita de Cochití,
no le hace que seiga indita
si al cabo no soy pa' ti.

Indita, indita, indita,
indita from another day,
where were you last night
that your belly is so cold?

Indita, indita, indita,
indita from another day,
where were you last night
that your belly is so cold?

Indita, indita, indita,
indita from Cochití,
it doesn't matter that you are Indian,
if in the end I'm not for you.

Indita, indita, indita,
indita from Cochití,
it doesn't matter that you are Indian,
if in the end I'm not for you.

On Friday, April 26, 1861, between the hours of 10 o'clock in the forenoon and 4 o'clock in the afternoon, Pablita Angel was sentenced to be hanged by the neck until dead for the murder of her lover, Juan Miguel Martín. She was to be taken by Sheriff Antonio Abade Herrera "to some suitable place … within one mile of the church within the town of Las Vegas" (New Mexico) where the sentence would be carried out.

It seems that the hapless Juan Miguel had decided to end his love affair with Pablita. She asked for a last meeting of farewell and during their final, fatal embrace, Pablita stabbed her lover below the left shoulder. Pablita was arraigned and tried by Judge Kirby Benedict, before whom she pleaded innocent. The judge found her guilty and sentenced her to death.

On the appointed day, Sheriff Herrera took his condemned prisoner to a cottonwood tree, stood

La finada Pablita

Performed by Julia Jaramillo

her in the back of a wagon, and slipped the noose over her head. He whipped away the team of horses, having forgotten to bind Pablita's wrists. The dangling woman desperately sought to avoid strangulation by holding onto the rope with her hands. The sheriff caught her by the waist and tried to use his own weight to finish the job. This proved too much for the assembled crowd, who stopped the proceeding and demanded her release. After a brief delay, Pablita was bound, placed back in the wagon, renoosed and hanged again, this time until dead, and was thus awarded the doubtful distinction of being the first woman to be legally executed in New Mexico.

This event became the subject of the *indita* entitled *La finada Pablita,* composed by Juan Ángel, a relative of the unfortunate woman. The following version of this classic was performed by Julia Jaramillo of Taos, New Mexico, who heard this song sung by both her mother and her aunt.

La finada Pablita	**The Late Pablita**
Julia Jaramillo	Julia Jaramillo
En el Río de Sapelló comenzó la suerte mía, en el Río de Sapelló comenzó la suerte mía.	On the river of Sapelló began my fate, On the river of Sapelló began my fate.
El Maldito me insistió a hacer tan grande avería, el Maldito me insistió a hacer tan grande avería.	The Evil one insisted that I cause such great damage, the Evil one insisted that I cause such great damage.
A Las Vegas me llevaran dice el aguacil mayor, a Las Vegas me llevaron, dice el aguacil mayor.	They will take me to Las Vegas the sheriff says, They took me to Las Vegas the sheriff says.

El cura me aconsejó
por el ejemplo miraron,
el cura me aconsejó
por el ejemplo miraron.

A muerte me sentenciaron
porque maté a Miguelito,
a muerte me sentenciaron
porque maté a Miguelito.

¿Madre mía pa' que tuvistes
una hija tan desgraciada,
madre mía pa' que tuvistes
una hija tan desgraciada?

Y de la prisión salí
con grillos encadenada,
y de la prisión salí
con grillos encadenada.

En el campo fui a morir
como los perros ahorcada,
en el campo fui a morir
como los perros ahorcada.

Adiós mis dos hermanitos,
échenme la bendición,
adiós mis dos hermanitos,
échenme la bendición.

Ruéguenle a Dios infinito
que mi alma tenga perdón,
ruéguenle a Dios infinito
que mi alma tenga perdón.

Santo Niñito de Atocha,
refugio de pecadores,
Santo Niñito de Atocha,
refugio de pecadores.

Por tu amada Madrecita,
sácame de estos clamores,
por tu amada Madrecita,
sácame de estos clamores.

Madre mía de los Dolores,
eres pura e infinita,
a quien oye mis clamores
como piadosa y bendita.

Madre mía de los Dolores,
eres pura e infinita,
a quien oye mis clamores
como piadosa y bendita.

The priest counseled me
my example they would see,
the priest counseled me
my example they would see.

They sentenced me to death
because I killed Miguelito,
They sentenced me to death
because I killed Miguelito.

Mother of mine, why did you have
such an unfortunate daughter?
Mother of mine, why did you have
such an unfortunate daughter?

And from prison I came out
chained with shackles,
and from prison I came out
chained with shackles.

In the countryside I went to die
hanged like a dog,
in the countryside I went to die
hanged like a dog.

Good-bye, my two little brothers,
give me your blessing,
good-bye, my two little brothers,
give me your blessing.

Beg infinite God
that my soul be pardoned,
beg infinite God
that my soul be pardoned.

Holy Child of Atocha,
refuge of sinners,
Holy Child of Atocha,
refuge of sinners.

Through your beloved Mother,
release me from these troubles,
through your beloved Mother,
release me from these troubles.

My Mother of Sorrows,
you are pure and infinite,
you who hear my troubles,
merciful and blessed.

My Mother of Sorrows,
you are pure and infinite,
you who hear my troubles,
merciful and blessed.

Indita de Manzano

Performed by Edwin Berry

Edwin Berry, the great folk singer of Tomé, New Mexico, sang a fine *indita* from Valencia County entitled *Indita de Manzano*. Señor Berry said that this tragic ballad mourns the death of José Luis Lobato, one of the most famous *músicos* of his time. The Indian girl mentioned in the ballad was a *genízara*, or captive. Señor Berry stated, "In New Mexico, there never was any real slavery. While there may have been some isolated cases of abuse or mistreatment (always repugnant), *inditas* or *inditos* were seen with favor and treated kindly, with love and decorum. They nearly always married into the family where they grew up. Poets chose to dedicate their songs to these adopted natives–the highest compliment they could give–a beautiful way to honor these orphans, indeed."

With regard to the song itself, Señor Berry went on to say, "It is a mystery how or why Lobato was mortally wounded. He couldn't speak. He was found by friends who met his horse, which led them to the dying man, a fine violinist still remembered in Belén, Tomé, Peralta, Chililí, and, of course, Manzano."

Señor Berry began this ballad by whistling an introductory melody in the key of B-flat major. Thereafter he changed the key to E-flat major and began singing the lyrics. The whistling continued to serve as an interlude dividing each of the four stanzas from the accompanying *estribillos*. He switched back and forth from B-flat major to E-flat major, ending the *indita* with the final whistled interlude. This is an unusual performance, in which Señor Berry accompanied himself on an Indian drum.

Indita de Manzano

Edwin Berry

Yo soy José Luis mentado
entre la flor y decencia,
soy el músico afamado
del condado de Valencia.

coro:
¡Ay, indita de Manzano,
ayuda a sentir,
pues fuiste tan afamada
con todo el mundo graciosa!
¡Y ay, José Luis,
y contigo desgraciada!

José Luis Lobato herido,
músico tan afamado,
tu cuerpo fue presentado
al condado de Valencia.

coro

Yo soy José Luis mentado
entre la gran competencia,
hoy va mi cuerpo tomado
al condado de Valencia.

coro

Little Indian Girl of Manzano

Edwin Berry

I am José Luis, well-known
in full flower and decency,
I am the famous musician
of the county of Valencia.

chorus:
Oh, little Indian girl of Manzano,
help us to mourn,
you have been so famous,
gracious to all the world!
Oh, José Luis,
and with you, so unfortunate!

José Luis Lobato mortally wounded,
such a famous musician,
your body was presented
to the county of Valencia.

chorus

I am José Luis, well-known
in the great competition,
today my body is taken
to the county of Valencia.

chorus

Adiós, José Luis querido,
pues fuiste tan afamado,
siempre serás admirado
por tu música y esencia.

coro

Farewell, beloved José Luis,
you were so famous.
You will always be admired
for your music and your spirit.

chorus

Some of the most fascinating *inditas* come from the Comanche celebrations that occur during the winter months across New Mexico. Nearly every Indian pueblo and several Hispano villages come alive with colorful processions and boisterous ceremonial dancing. Other Hispano villages feature heroic historical dramas and religious morality plays; all in mixed defiance and emulation of a much-admired former foe–those Yamparicas, Yupes, Cuchanecas, and Ietanes known collectively as Nuhmuhnuh "los comanches," a Shoshonean people who militarily dominated New Mexico in the eighteenth century.

Prior to World War II, fieldworkers such as Reyes Martínez and Loren Brown observed that several Hispano communities (among them Ranchos de Taos) celebrated the complete cycle of Comanche celebrations, including "Los comanches de castillo," the eighteenth-century heroic military play, the nativity play entitled "Los comanches," and Comanche music and costumed

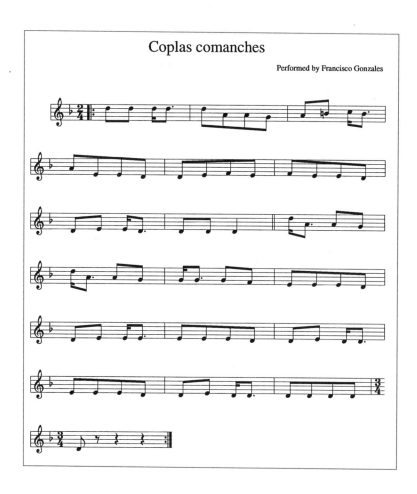

Coplas comanches

Performed by Francisco Gonzales

dancing used for the feast of Manuel (January 1), the feast of the Conversion of San Pablo (January 25), and for family events such as weddings and baptisms. This cluster of celebrations has since fragmented, with Ranchos de Taos as the primary site of Comanche music and dancing, Alcalde as the last home for the military play, and Bernalillo as one of the last communities in which portions of the nativity play are performed.

Although the Hispano singers and dancers of Ranchos de Taos identify themselves and their tradition as "Comanche," their music has strong Pueblo and Navajo influences and only a couple of songs that the Nuhmuhnuh or Oklahoma Comanches would recognize. The energetic dancing is in the contemporary Pow Wow tradition. Historical references in the lyrics, however, can be traced to the late eighteenth century, when Taos was a major center of Comanche contact, both commerce and depredations.

The most prominent Comanche families include the Mondragón, Durán, Frézquez, Archuleta, Struck, and Gonzales clans. Francisco "El Comanche" Gonzales has dedicated much of his energy to the celebration of his *genízaro* heritage. His repertory includes almost two dozen songs and dances. Most of the songs are sung in "vocables," the syllable singing typical of Native American music. However, several of the songs have lyrics in Spanish. The themes of burlesque love and warfare are common in other New Mexican *inditas*. The last verse concerning the starving Comanche couple exchanging their children for food strikes a tragic note as well.

Coplas comanches	Comanche Verses
Francisco "El Comanche" Gonzales	Francisco "El Comanche" Gonzales

Anteanoche fui a tu casa	The night before last I went to your house
y me dites de cenar,	and you gave me dinner,
tortillitas chamuscadas	little burned tortillas
y frijoles sin guisar.	and uncooked beans.
coro:	*chorus:*
Epa nava, ene yo,	*Epa nava, ene yo,*
saca navajo, jeyó,	*saca navajo, heyo,*
ya yo jene ya jeyó,	*ya yo hene ya heyo,*
ya yo jeyo jeieieieio.	*ya yo heyo heieieieio.*
El comanche y el apache	The Comanche and the Apache
se citaron una guerra,	made a date for battle,
el comanche no se raja	the Comanche doesn't give in
y el apache se le aferra.	and the Apache bears down harder.
coro	*chorus*
Si tu andas en combate	If you are in combat
y tu tropa no ganó,	and your troops lost,
pide a Dios que te rescate,	beg God to rescue you
si el enemigo es navajó.	if the enemy is Navajo.
coro	*chorus*

Cuando vayas pa' navajó,	If you would go to Navajo land
aprevente del mortal,	beware of the danger,
porque la muerte de allá,	because death from over there
es firme y no se rebaja.	is firm and unyielding.
coro	*chorus*
El comanche y la comancha	The Comanche and his wife
se fueron pa' Santa Fe,	went to Santa Fe,
a vender a sus hijitos	to sell their children
por harina y por café.	for flour and coffee.
coro	*chorus*

While the ancestors of the Pueblo Indians have lived for millennia in what is currently regarded as the southwestern United States, the Athabascans apparently arrived in this region only shortly before the Spaniards. Whereas the Spaniards penetrated the region of the Río Grande del Norte questing for gold, the Athabascans moved in from the north in pursuit of their lifestyle, following game trails and raiding the sedentary Pueblos. They left relatives in their wake whose descendants may be recognized through the science of linguistics. These Indians were raiders and hunter-gatherers, unlike the more peaceful agrarian Puebloans. The Navajos and Apaches stole horses from the Spaniards and became formidable horsemen in their own right. The Navajos remained close to the San Juan River, while the different groups of Apaches selected territories throughout what are now New Mexico and Arizona. The Spanish came to regard Apache raids as natural disasters to be endured and survived if possible.

As time wore on and territories became established, one area along the Río Grande was defined as Apache country and was entered only with great caution. The Río Grande north of El Paso del Norte was dominated on the east by Mescalero Apaches and to the west by Chiricahua Apaches, who were regarded as extraordinary warriors and "one of the toughest human species the world has ever known." The presence of Apaches and the extreme aridity of the region were definitely major factors contributing to the relatively late settling of the area.

The Apaches held sway over much of this landscape until well into the latter decades of the nineteenth century. Accounts of Apache raids are still recounted by individuals whose parents and grandparents came face to face with hostile Apaches. Juan De La O was born in Salem, New Mexico, north of Doña Ana, about the time the dust was settling after the long period of Apache raids. Two of his grand-uncles were killed by Victorio, a well-known and greatly feared Apache leader. Señor De La O said, "Victorio hung around where I was born between Las Cruces and that territory. In fact, Victorio and his men killed two of my dad's uncles—right above Hatch—Cerro de las Uvas ["Hill of the Grapes"]—My two great uncles were killed there …" Señor De La O went on to say, "Victorio wasn't no Indian. He was Spanish, he was what they call *cautivo*. *Cautivo* was a little boy that the Indians used to kidnap and take with them. And he was raised with Indians. They took him as a little boy. And he was meaner than the Indians. Yes, because some of my old folks knew him and he was no Indian. He had a white beard this long. Even blue eyes. Because I knew an old man who met face to face with him. They were going to fight with him and the leader of this bunch of Spanish people were going to meet with him. And Victorio came from this way and that man came from that way. And he was no Indian."

Señor De La O spent much of his adult life as a professional violinist, bassist, guitarist, and vocalist. He is remembered by many older generation Hispanos for his performances of traditional music around Albuquerque. Juan De La O performed two *inditas* included here, *El indio Manuel,* a burlesque *indita* about the famous Navajo chieftain, Manuelito, and in a more heroic vein, *El indio Victorio.*

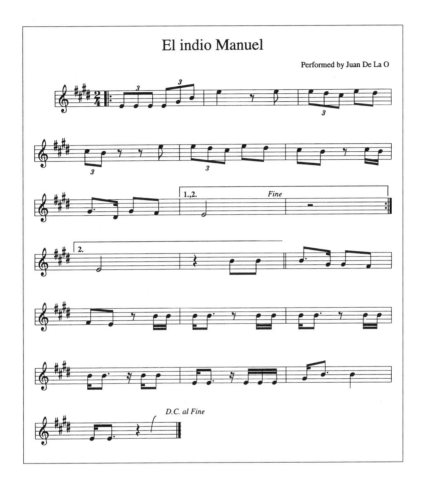

El indio Manuel

Juan De La O

Yo soy el indio Manuel,
hermanito de Mariano,
y con mi flecha en la mano
empalmo de a dos en tres.

Yo soy el indio Manuel,
hermanito de Mariano,
y con mi flecha en la mano
empalmo de a dos en tres.

The Indian Manuel

Juan De La O

I am the Indian Manuel,
little brother of Mariano,
and with my arrow in my hand
I dispatch two to three.

I am the Indian Manuel,
little brother of Mariano,
and with my arrow in my hand
I dispatch two to three.

Cuando salí de mi tierra
con ganas de jinetear,
me subí en un macho muerto
y no me pudo tumbar.

Pobrecita mi abuelita,
tanta fama que me daba,
le clavaban las espuelas
el macho ni se meneaba.

Cuando salí de mi tierra
de nadie me despedí,
no más de los tinamaistes
y un gato que estaba allí.

Pobrecita mi abuelita,
tanta fama que me daba,
le clavaban las espuelas
el macho ni se meneaba.

When I left my land
wanting to ride on horseback,
I mounted a dead mule
that couldn't throw me.

My poor grandmother,
so much fame she gave me,
the spurs dug in so hard
the mule didn't even wiggle.

When I left my land,
I didn't bid farewell to anyone,
except some cooking irons,
and a cat that was there.

My poor grandmother,
so much fame she gave me,
the spurs dug in so hard
the mule didn't even wiggle.

El indio Victorio

Juan De La O

Yo soy el indio Victorio,
mi profesión es matar,
es mi vida y es mi gloria
hacer al mundo temblar.

Quiero morir, quiero vivir,
no quiero morir sin mi deber.

Victorio empuñó su espada
para combatir el estado.
Varias vidas me tomé
y allí también algún ganado.

Quiero morir, quiero vivir,
no quiero morir sin mi deber.

The Indian Victorio

Juan De La O

I am the Indian Victorio,
killing is my profession,
it is my life and my glory
to make the world tremble.

I want to die, I want to live,
I don't want to die without my duty.

Victorio took up his sword
to combat the state.
I have taken several lives
and some cattle there also.

I want to die, I want to live,
I don't want to die without my duty.

El indio Victorio

Performed by Juan De La O

A form of *indita* that reflects the dangers of life on the frontier is the *cautiva,* or captive song. Robb states that a form of *cautiva* exists in Spain, dating from the time when Moors took Spanish captives prior to their final expulsion from Spain in 1492. One of the best known of the New Mexican *cautivas* is *La cautiva Marcelina,* which recounts the tragic tale of Indians taking a young woman captive. Marcelina witnesses the death of her father, her brothers, and her children at the hands of her captors. In a version of this ballad that appears in Robb's opus, Marcelina was being taken to the region of the Río Huicho, passing Puertecito and the Río Grande. Both of Robb's versions differ textually from the version presented here; however, the melody lines are quite similar, indicating that these three are permutations of the same *cautiva.*

The following version was sung and played by Señora Virginia Bernal of Ratón, New Mexico. In western New Mexico, this *indita* was often sung as part of a nativity play entitled "Los comanches," in which a group of Indians portrayed by Hispano villagers come to dance for the infant Jesus, then take him away as a captive. Another *indita* from this play is discussed in the chapter on *teatro popular,* or folk theater.

La cautiva Marcelina	**Marcelina, the Captive**
Virginia Bernal	Virginia Bernal
La cautiva Marcelina	Marcelina, the captive,
ya se va, ya se la llevan,	now she's leaving, they're taking her away,
ya se va, ya se la llevan	now she's leaving, they're taking her away
para esas tierras mentadas	to those famous lands,
a comer carne de yegua,	to eat mare's meat,
a comer carne de yegua.	to eat mare's meat.

refrán:
Por eso ya no quiero
en el mundo más amar,
de mi querida patria
me van a retirar.

La cautiva Marcelina
cuando llegó al aguapá,
cuando llegó al aguapá
volteó la cara llorando,
"Mataron a mi papá,
mataron a mi papá."

refrán

La cautiva Marcelina
cuando ya llegó a los llanos,
cuando ya llegó a los llanos
volteó la cara llorando,
"Mataron a mis hermanos
mataron a mis hermanos."

refrán

La cautiva Marcelina
cuando llegó al ojito,
cuando llegó al ojito
volteó la cara llorando,
"Mataron al Delgadito,
mataron al Delgadito."

refrán

La cautiva Marcelina
cuando llegó a los cerritos,
cuando llegó a los cerritos
volteó la cara llorando,
"Mataron a mis hijitos,
mataron a mis hijitos."

refrán

chorus:
That's why I no longer
want to love in this world,
from my beloved homeland
they are taking me away.

Marcelina, the captive,
when she arrived at the cattail marsh,
when she arrived at the cattail marsh,
she looked back crying,
"They killed my father,
they killed my father."

chorus

Marcelina, the captive,
when she came to the plains,
when she came to the plains,
she looked back crying,
"They killed my brothers,
they killed my brothers."

chorus

Marcelina, the captive,
when she arrived at the spring,
when she arrived at the spring,
she looked back crying,
"They killed Delgadito,
they killed Delgadito."

chorus

Marcelina, the captive,
when she arrived at the hills,
when she arrived at the hills,
she looked back crying,
"They killed my children,
they killed my children."

chorus

La cautiva Marcelina

Performed by Virginia Bernal

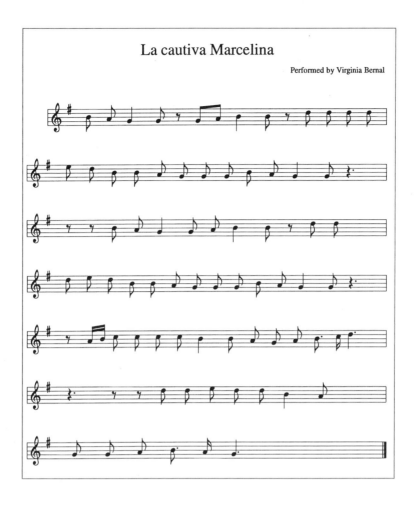

CHAPTER THREE

Corridos

A s the Spanish colonists and their descendants focused their energy on surviving in a New World, their Iberian memories became ever more remote. Although they were aware of their cultural origins, their consciousness was molded by the environment that surrounded them. Their narrative ballads reflect this shift in attitude. The *romances* tout the deeds of the aristocracy and in some instances recall the presence of a hero well beyond the span of his mortality. The narrative ballad also provided a medium of expression for the recollection of an event. Thus the *romance* set the precedent for the *corrido,* which met the needs of an active and self-directed people who were forced to document their own experience of history.

The *corrido* as we know it was performed in Mexico in the mid-nineteenth century but may have evolved even earlier. It has subsequently become a musical form of enormous proportions. The great Mexican ethnomusicologist Vicente Mendoza traced this form to the *romance*; Mendoza says, "The Mexican *corrido,* a completely popular form . . . is an expression of the sensibility of our people, and its direct ancestor, both literary and musical, is the Spanish *romance.*" The *corrido* expresses events in the lives of ordinary people, events that are frequently violent or tragic. They express the dark side of existence by chronicling everyday disasters. The *corrido* is a means of externalizing the despair of death and misfortune while attempting to keep everything in human perspective. Considered in this light, it is interesting to note that *corridos* are almost always performed in a major rather than minor mode. The central debate on the evolution and spread of the *corrido* was between Mendoza, who believed that it originated in central Mexico and spread northward, and Américo Paredes, who argued convincingly that the *corrido* developed along the United States–Mexico borderlands and spread south.

Corridos usually include the date and time of the event described and often the name of the composer. Sometimes they end in a *despedida,* or concluding refrain, with the words, "*Vuela, vuela palomita . . . ,*" "Fly, fly little dove . . ." The *corrido* is generally comprised of *cuartetas,* or quatrains, four *versos* of eight syllables each, whereas the verso of the *romance* is of sixteen syllables. Both the *corrido* and the *romance* have stanzas of thirty-two syllables. The guitar is the instrument most widely used to accompany the singing of these ballads.

Many of the *corridos,* especially of Mexican origin, are sung in a harmony of thirds. One possible origin is the Franciscan clerics' instruction of the Indians in simple harmony of a third above or a sixth below the *cantus firmus,* or melody line; this tradition prevailed among native musicians for centuries.

During the Mexican Revolution, the *corrido* became something of a journalistic device whereby the people were kept informed of recent events and popular opinions about them. Geijerstam states that the history of Mexico may be traced from the mid-nineteenth century in the texts of *corridos*. It is evident that many of the *corridos* extolled the exploits of the leaders of the revolution and were the music of *la gente*, not the aristocracy. Many of the *corridos* of the revolution were printed as broadsides and illustrated by engravings of the celebrated artist José Guadalupe Posada (1852–1913).

During this period professional *corridistas* accompanied revolutionary soldiers into combat zones as musical chroniclers. The most famous of these is reputed to have been Samuel M. Lozano, who, for a period of time, was the personal *corridista* for Pancho Villa.

The *corrido* attained great popularity north of the border for a span of well over a century, although this popularity has waned somewhat with the rise of *rancheras* and *música norteña* (Mexico's "country music") as well as pop and rock and roll. Many of the Mexican *corridos* became firmly implanted in the musical tradition of the Río Grande del Norte, and to this day Pancho Villa is conceivably the most popular folk hero in this region. There are *corridos* of New Mexican provenance, but generally they are not as widely popular as the Mexican *corridos*.

A *corrido* that has been well known in the Río Grande del Norte for at least fifty years is entitled *Contrabando de El Paso*, which tells the plight of a bootlegger caught smuggling tequila across the Río Grande who was sentenced to prison in Leavenworth, Kansas. The original *corrido* is nearly twenty stanzas long, and the version presented here is greatly abbreviated. As Robb wryly points out, the *prisionero* rues not that he broke the law, but rather that he was apprehended at such a delightfully lucrative profession. This is the basis for a point of view shared by many who question the imposition of authority by a governing body that is itself suspect.

An important consideration here is that the Río Grande is first and foremost a river in an arid landscape whose inhabitants look to the flow of water as life-sustaining. To those who live close to this land, it is an unnatural thought to regard the Río Grande as a geopolitical boundary. Américo Paredes aptly indicates that for generations, people living on either side of the river regarded each other as neighbors and thought nothing of wading across the river, often bearing gifts. Within the purview of the prevailing bureaucracy, this could be construed both as illegal visitation and smuggling. While rafting the lower canyons of the Río Grande, I have witnessed smugglers who wander at will back and forth across the river, cheerfully bearing their contraband. I have had smugglers come to my campfire for a plate of beans or to sit for a spell. In my experience they are interesting and extremely conscious of following a picaresque tradition based on a system of honor that is intuited rather than legislated.

The version of *Contrabando de El Paso* presented here was performed by the late Señor Ventura Rael, who was born in Mimbres, New Mexico. Señor Rael was regarded as one of the great *Nuevo Mexicano* fiddlers. He accompanied himself on a guitar he had borrowed from his friend, Crescencio M. García, who performed the version of *Delgadina* included in this work. Señor Rael was seventy-nine years old at the time of recording.

Enrique R. Lamadrid notes that the translation of *mañanas* here is "morning ballad." From the Mexican tradition, the *mañanita* is a commemorative song used on ceremonial occasions, and often sung in the early morning. Some *corrido* ballads are called *mañanitas*. The best known of all the *mañanitas* is the one sung for birthdays.

Contrabando de El Paso

Performed by Ventura Rael

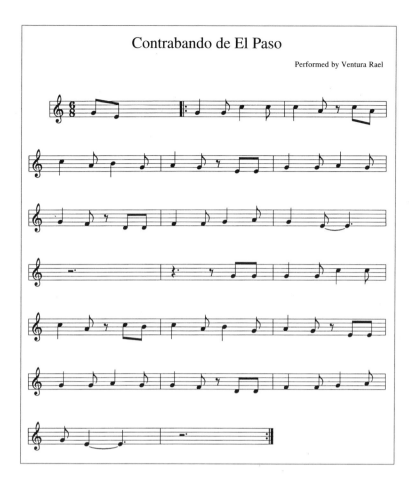

Contrabando de El Paso

Ventura Rael

Sí, es bonito el contrabando,
se gana mucho dinero,
pero lo que mal me puede
las penas del prisionero.

Víspera de San Lorenzo
como a las once del día
recumbraban los umbrales
de la penitenciaría.

Unos vienen con un año,
otros con diez y ocho meses,
otros con un año y un día,
a la penitenciaría.

Ya allí viene silbando el tren,
ya no tardará en llegar
yo les digo a mis amigos
que no vayan a llorar.

Contraband of El Paso

Ventura Rael

Yes, contraband is beautiful,
one can earn a lot of money,
but that which is bad is
the pain of being a prisoner.

On the eve of San Lorenzo
about eleven that day,
loomed the thresholds
of the penitentiary.

Some arrive with a year,
others with eighteen months,
others with a year and a day
to the penitentiary.

Now the whistling train is coming,
it won't be long in arriving,
I tell my friends,
not to go and cry.

Unos vienen con un año, otros con diez y ocho meses, otros con un año y un día, a la penitenciaría.	Some arrive with a year, others with eighteen months, others with a year and a day to the penitentiary.
Y ahí te mando, mamacita, un suspiro y un abrazo, pa' que te canta las mañanas del contrabando del Paso.	Oh, mother, there I send you a sigh and a hug, so I can sing you the ballad of the contraband of El Paso.

*O*ne of the most famous of the *corridos* to have originated in New Mexico is entitled *El corrido de San Marcial*. In 1929 and again in 1937, the Río Grande flooded its banks and inundated the town of San Marcial, which was located about twenty-five miles south of Socorro, New Mexico. Earlier in the century, the Elephant Butte Dam was constructed near the town of what is now called Truth or Consequences, which resulted in Elephant Butte Lake, fed by the Río Grande. In 1929 and 1937 there were unusual amounts of rain, and the lake filled at an inordinate rate. Sand and silt backed up for miles because of slower currents. The people of that region as well as scientists have expressed the contention that if not for the dam, San Marcial would have been spared. San Marcial had been a thriving community and a center for the railroad. There was a Fred Harvey restaurant and a local population of a few thousand. After the second flooding, the residents abandoned San Marcial. Ironically the U.S. Army Corps of Engineers who built the dam touted the construction as a flood control project. Ramón Luna wrote the New Mexican classic, *El corrido de San Marcial*.

Roger Gabaldón and Manuel Rosas spent their boyhoods in San Marcial and have remained friends for life. As youngsters they sang together, and in 1979 they consented to sing some of the *corridos* of their youth, including *El corrido de San Marcial*.

El corrido de San Marcial

Written by Ramón Luna
Performed by Manuel Rosas and Roger Gabaldón

El corrido de San Marcial

Manuel Rosas & Roger Gabaldón

El día veinte de agosto
no me quisiera acordar,
que se llegó el Río Grande
a la plaza de San Marcial.

Era una tarde muy triste
fecha la tengo presente,
trenes llegaron de El Paso
para auxiliar a la gente.

La gente andaba asustada
si no hallaba qué pensar,
si marcharse para El Paso
o quedarse en San Marcial.

Pobrecita de mi gente,
¡ay, qué suerte les tocó!
Todas sus casas perdieron
no más el Harvey quedó.

¡Ay, qué lástima de pueblo
cómo quedó destrozado!
Por en medio de las calles,
lomas de arena quedaron.

No soy trovador ni poeta
no tengo ninguna gracia,
pero sí pude trovarle
este corrido a mi plaza.

Le compuse este corrido
a los paisanos de aquí,
voy a decirles mi nombre
para que se acuerden de mí.

Pues mi nombre es Ramón Luna,
yo soy nacido de aquí,
y es porque a mí me duele
la plaza donde nací.

Ya me voy a despedir
las gracias les voy a dar,
aquí se acabó el corrido
del final de San Marcial.

Corrido of San Marcial

Manuel Rosas & Roger Gabaldón

On the 20th of August,
I don't like to remember it,
the Río Grande flooded
the town of San Marcial.

It was a sad afternoon
on that date I remember,
that trains arrived from El Paso
to help the people.

The people were wandering frightened
and didn't know what to think,
whether to go to El Paso
or remain in San Marcial.

My poor people,
oh, what misfortune befell them!
All their houses were lost,
and only the Harvey House remained.

Oh, what a pitiful town,
how it was ruined!
In the middle of all the streets,
hills of sand remained.

I am no troubadour nor poet,
no wit nor charm have I,
but yes, I was able to sing
this ballad for my town.

I composed this corrido
for my countrymen from here,
I will tell them my name
so that they will remember me.

Well, my name is Ramón Luna
and I was born here,
and it's because I feel compassion
for the place where I was born.

Now I will bid farewell,
and will give thanks to you,
here ends the ballad
of the end of San Marcial.

Mexico is rich with *corridos,* many of which are sung north of the border. One *corrido* from Mexico that has been known in the Río Grande del Norte for many years is *El hijo desobediente.* Vicente Mendoza listed this *corrido* as a *maldición,* inasmuch as the disobedient son was cursed by his father. Aurora Lucero-White classified it as a *tragedia.* She also predicted in 1953 that this *corrido* would enjoy a long life because of its universality. Indeed it is still sung throughout the region.

The version of *El hijo desobediente* presented here was performed by Floyd Aguilar of Springer, New Mexico. It is almost identical to a version published in *Cancionero Fiesta,* edited by Pedro Ribero-Ortega and is similar to a version recorded by Terrence Hansen in California in 1959, which was included in Robb's opus. Between parentheses are key portions of the text and story line that the singer left out of our recorded version.

El hijo desobediente

Floyd Aguilar

Un domingo estando errando
se encontraron dos mancebos
metiendo mano a sus fierros
como queriendo pelear.

Cuando se estaban peleando
pues llegó su padre de uno,
"Hijo de mi corazón,
ya no pelees con ninguno."

"Cuando (Quítese de) aquí, mi padre,
estoy más bravo que un león,
no vaya a sacar mi espada,
le traspasé el corazón."

"Hijo de mi corazón,
por lo que acabas de hablar
antes de que raye el sol,
la vida te han de quitar."

Lo que le pido a mi padre
que no me entierre en sagrado
que me entierre en tierra bruta
donde me trille el ganado.

Con una mano de fuera
y un papel sobre dorado
con un letrero que diga
"Felipe fue desgraciado."

The Disobedient Son

Floyd Aguilar

One Sunday while wandering around
two young men met
and reached for their steel
as if wanting to fight.

When they were fighting
the father of one arrived,
"Son of my heart,
don't fight with anyone."

"(Get out of here,) my father,
I am more fierce than a lion,
don't pull out my sword,
I have pierced his heart through."

"Son of my heart,
for what you have just said,
before the sun rises
they will take your life."

What I ask of my father
is not to bury me in sacred ground,
but to bury me in the wild lands
where the cattle will thresh over me.

With fancy handwriting
on paper stamped with gold,
with an inscription reading
"Felipe was unfortunate."

Mi caballo colorado hace un año que nació, allí se lo dejo a mi padre por la crianza que me dio.	My roan horse that was born a year ago, I leave to my father for raising me.
De tres caballos que tengo, allí se los dejo a los pobres para que siquiera digan, Felipe, Dios te perdone.	Of the three horses I have, I leave them to the poor so they'll at least say, Felipe, may God forgive you.
Bajaron el toro prieto que nunca lo habían bajado, pero ahora sí ya bajó revuelto con el ganado.	They brought down the black bull that had never been down before, but now he is down among all the cattle.
(Y a ese mentado Felipe la maldición le alcanzó y en las trancas del corral el toro se lo llevó.)	(And that renowned Felipe, the curse reached him, on the gate of the corral the bull took his life.)
Ya con esta me despido con la estrella de oriente. Esto les puede pasar, al hijo desobediente.	Now with this I bid farewell, with the eastern star. This can happen to you, to a disobedient son.

El hijo desobediente

Performed by Floyd Aguilar

Even though the internal combustion engine has exhaustively insinuated itself into the heart of Western culture and beyond, the horse remains in a state of symbiosis with *la gente* on both sides of the international boundary. One of the many ways Mendoza classified *corridos* involved horses, which have traditionally captured an enormous amount of attention within the collective psyche of *la gente*.

One such *corrido* is entitled *El potro "Lobo Gatiado,"* which is reputed by Mario Colín to have come from Tlatlaya, Mexico, and which tells the tale of a mean stud pitted in a high-stakes horse race against a red mare. The title *"Lobo Gatiado"* seems to suggest a translation something like "Catty Wolf," but Enrique R. Lamadrid heard from a Texas *vaquero* that *"Lobo Gatiado"* is a corruption of the term *"lomo goteado,"* or spotted shoulders, one of the characteristic markings of the Appaloosa breed.

This version of *El potro "Lobo Gatiado"* was performed by Rumaldo Guilez and his son Chon. Rumaldo Guilez sings in a characteristic high tenor style much in demand in earlier days among *la gente*. The Guilez family lives in Tularosa, New Mexico, east of the Tularosa Basin, where the first atomic bomb was detonated in 1945.

El potro "Lobo Gatiado"

Rumaldo & Chon Guilez

En una manada vide
un potro que me gustaba,
me fui con el hacendado,
"Señor, traigo una tratada,
quiero que me dé un caballo
por mi yegua colorada."

"¿Qué caballo es el que quieres
por fin de poder tratar?"
"Un potro lobo y gatiado
que ayer vide en el corral,
que charros y caporales
no lo han podido amansar."

"Ese caballo que quieres
pensaba yo echarlo al carro,
por la yegua doy quinientos,
el potro te lo regalo,
que charros y caporales
a todos los ha tumbado."

Pues luego que ya trataron
el mismo le echó la hablada,
"Si mi caballo le corre
a su yegua colorada,
con dos mil quinientos pesos
ya se acerca la jugada."

The Horse "Lobo Gatiado"

Rumaldo & Chon Guilez

In a herd I saw
a colt that I liked,
I went to see the rancher,
"Señor, I bring you a deal,
I want you to give me a colt
in exchange for my roan mare."

"Which horse is the one you want
for the purpose of this deal?"
"The colt, 'Lobo Gatiado,'
that I saw yesterday in the corral,
who wranglers and foremen
could not tame."

"That colt that you want
I was thinking of hitching to a wagon,
for the mare I'll pay five hundred,
and I'll give you that colt
who threw wranglers and foremen
and everyone else."

Well as soon as they made the trade
the same one voiced his challenge,
"If my colt runs
against your roan mare,
with two thousand five hundred pesos
the race is approaching."

El potro "Lobo Gatiado"

Performed by Rumaldo y Chon Guilez

Me contestó el hacendado,	The rancher answered me,
"No digas que tengo miedo,	"Don't say that I am afraid,
vámonos a la oficina	let's go to the office
a depositar el dinero,	to deposit the money,
la carrera la corremos	we'll run the race
el veinte y tres de febrero."	on the twenty-third of February."
Se llegó el dichoso día	The lucky day arrived
de la carrera afamada,	for the famous race,
yo veía pesos tronchados	I saw pesos thrown down
a la yegua colorada,	on the roan mare,
y al potro Lobo Gatiado	and on "Lobo Gatiado"
ni quien le apostara nada.	nobody bet anything.
"Apuéstenle a mi caballo,	"Come, bet on my colt,
mi caballo es muy bonito,	my colt is very beautiful,
nadie lo quería por duro,	nobody wanted him for being tough,
lo duro yo se lo quito,"	but I'll take away his toughness,"
y a poco tiempo lo vieron	and not too long after they saw him
arrendándose solito.	reining himself.
Pues dieron la voz de arranque,	They shouted to start,
al cabo allí no se vio,	finally nothing could be seen,
se cubrió de polvadera,	a dust cloud covered everything,
¡ya qué animal tan violento!	what a violent animal!
No más alas le faltaban	All he lacked were wings
para volar por el viento.	to fly through the wind.

Pues dieron la voz de arranque,	Well, they shouted to start,
la yegua se adelantó,	the roan mare pulled ahead,
el potro "gatiado"	the colt "Gatiado"
al disparo se quedó,	stalled at the gun,
al salir a la otra orilla	but on reaching the other end,
con dos cuerpos le ganó.	he won by two lengths.

Ya con esta me despido,	With this I bid farewell,
dispense lo mal trovado,	forgive the bad singing,
aquí termina el corrido	here ends the ballad
de un charro y un hacendado,	of a cowboy and a rancher,
de la yegua colorada	of the roan mare
y el potro "Lobo Gatiado."	and the colt "Lobo Gatiado."

Mexican *corridos* spread like the wind during the many years of the Mexican Revolution. The heroes of the revolution were immortalized in *coplas* composed by *corridistas* who observed battles and then recorded their observations in poetry. Two of the most celebrated heroes of the Mexican Revolution were Emiliano Zapata, from the south of Mexico, and Pancho Villa, the great general from the north.

Francisco Villa was originally named Doroteo Arango. When he was a young man of seventeen, he had already become an outlaw for having shot a man who had molested his sister. He assumed his grandfather's surname, thereafter calling himself Francisco Villa. For some time he led the life of an outlaw, eluding the *rurales,* or federal rural police, who were bent on capturing him. In time he became a revolutionary and was known as "the centaur of the north." He was famous for his unpredictable temper, his arbitrary cruelty, and his brilliant battle tactics. In 1916 he raided the town of Columbus, New Mexico, which resulted in an unsuccessful campaign mounted by the U.S. Army under the command of General John "Black Jack" Pershing, who followed the trail of Villa throughout northern Mexico to no avail. This fruitless campaign marked the first use of automobiles and airplanes by the military, a meager preface to the mighty conflict which was to follow during World War I.

We have included two *corridos de la revolución* in the present work. The first is entitled *Del fusilamiento del General Felipe Ángeles.* Felipe Ángeles was a brilliant strategist and master artilleryman who worked closely with Pancho Villa. He was a man of refined sensibilities, educated in both France and at the Colegio Militar in Mexico. He was an aristocrat with a conscience and readily perceived the grim reality of the lives of the *peones,* or peasants. He was forced to leave Mexico when Pancho Villa's army was disbanded. He returned to Mexico to fight the forces of Carranza and was ultimately captured. On July 26, 1919, he was shot "through the heart" at his insistence before a firing squad, a heroic detail of the *corrido.*

The version of *Del fusilamiento del Felipe Ángeles* presented here was performed by Juan Manuel "Johnny" Flórez and Raúl García of Las Cruces, New Mexico. Señores Flórez y García are two of the greatest performers of the Mexican *corrido* in the region of the Río Grande del Norte.

El corrido del fusilamiento de Felipe Angeles

Performed by Juan Manuel Flórez and Raúl García

El corrido del fusilamiento de Felipe Ángeles

Johnny Floréz & Raúl García

En mil novecientos veinte,
señores, tengan presente,
fusilaron en Chihuahua
a un general muy valiente.

En el cerro de La Mora,
le tocó la mala suerte,
lo tomaron prisionero,
lo sentenciaron a muerte.

Ángeles mandó un escrito
al congreso de la unión,
pa' ver si le perdonaban
y alcanzaba salvación.

Pero no le permitieron
por ser un reo militar.
Le dijo a sus compañeros,
"Ya me van a fusilar."

Cantaba una palomita
cuando estaba prisionero,
se acordaba de su tiempo
cuando él era guerrillero.

De a guerrero comenzó
su carrera militar,
dentro de poquito tiempo
llegó a ser un general.

The Execution of Felipe Ángeles

Johnny Floréz & Raúl García

In the year 1920,
señores, please recall,
they shot in Chihuahua
a very brave general.

On the hill at La Mora
ill fate struck,
they took him prisoner
and sentenced him to death.

Ángeles sent a petition
to the congress of the union,
to see if they would pardon him
and so gain his salvation.

But they would not permit it
since he was a criminal of war.
He said to his companions,
"Now they are going to shoot me."

A dove was singing
when he was a prisoner,
he remembered the time
when he was a soldier.

As a soldier he began
his military career,
before too long
he became a general.

El reloj marca sus horas	The clock marks its hours,
se llega la reclusión,	the final confinement arrives,
"Preparen muy bien sus armas	"Prepare your arms well,
apúntenme al corazón."	and aim at my heart."
"Yo no soy de los cobardes	"I'm not one of those cowards
que le temen a la muerte,	that fears death,
la muerte no mata a nadie,	death does not kill anyone,
la matadora es la suerte."	the killer is fate."
Ya con esta me despido,	With this I bid you farewell,
por las hojas de un nogal,	through the leaves of a walnut tree,
fusilaron en Chihuahua	in Chihuahua they shot
a un valiente general.	a brave general.

Benjamín Argumedo was another revolutionary figure whose name is remembered by those who sing the *corrido* that recounts the circumstances of his execution. Born in Matamoros, Coahuila, he was regarded as a fearless cavalryman. Beginning in 1910 Argumedo served under a succession of revolutionary leaders including Madero, Orozco, Huerta, and Zapata. His shift of allegiance from Madero to Orozco reflects his ambitious nature. He finally attained the rank of general before his final, fatal capture in Durango.

The years of the Mexican Revolution were a mosaic of intrigue. Ostensibly the revolutionary heroes were leading the people of Mexico in revolt against an oligarchy that had remained entrenched for decades. However, a power struggle among revolutionary leaders resulted in the bitter proof that power corrupts even those whose origins reflect some sense of altruism. Men such as Zapata and Ángeles displayed a level of integrity that was indeed uncommon. Others, including Villa himself, are regarded by some as having used the revolution to work out their own fantasies regardless of the bloodshed and misery.

As Américo Paredes points out, the term *mañanitas* is applied to *corridos* that recount the circumstances of the execution of a great military leader. These ballads reflect the courage and stoicism displayed by men such as Felipe Ángeles and Benjamín Argumedo. Argumedo's final request was that he be executed in the plaza in the presence of the people whose rights he defended; however, this request was denied by his executioner, General Francisco Murguía. And so on February

Las mañanitas de Benjamín Argumedo

Performed by Librado Tórrez

29, 1916, Benjamín Argumedo met his destiny blindfolded and tied to a chair before a firing squad. He was so ill at the time that he could no longer stand. His final message to the world was that no one should make a display of wealth and status, because " … we are all equal material for the grave."

The version of *Las mañanitas de Benjamín Argumedo* presented here is somewhat abbreviated. A complete text of this *corrido* may be found in *El corrido mexicano,* by Vicente T. Mendoza. Our version was performed by Librado Tórrez of Carrizozo, New Mexico, who was eighty-six years old at the time the recording was made.

Las mañanitas de Benjamín Argumedo

Librado Tórrez

Para empezar a cantar,
para empezar a cantar,
pido el permiso primero.
Señores, son las mañanas,
señores son las mañanas
de Benjamín Argumedo.

¿Dónde se encuentra Argumedo,
dónde se encuentra Argumedo,
que tiene el camino andado,
y en no hallar su caballo
a orillas de una laguna?

Salieron con Argumedo,
salieron con Argumedo
en un carro como flete.
Pasaron por San Miguel,
pasaron por San Miguel,
llegaron a Sombrerete.

Tanto pelear y pelear,
tanto pelear y pelear
con mi Mauser en las manos.
Vine a morir fusilado,
vine a morir fusilado
en el panteón de Durango.

"Óigame usted, general,
óigame usted, general,
también yo soy hombre valiente.
Quiero que usted a mí fusile,
quiero que usted a mí fusile
y al público de la gente."

The Ballad of Benjamín Argumedo

Librado Tórrez

In order to begin singing,
in order to begin singing,
first I ask permission.
Señores, this is the ballad,
señores, this is the ballad
of Benjamín Argumedo.

Where can Argumedo be found,
where can Argumedo be found?
He has walked down the road,
not finding his horse
on the shores of a lake.

They left with Argumedo,
they left with Argumedo
like baggage in a boxcar.
They passed through San Miguel,
they passed through San Miguel
and arrived at Sombrerete.

So much fighting and fighting,
so much fighting and fighting
with my Mauser in my hands.
I came to be shot,
I came to be shot
in the cemetery of Durango.

"Listen to me, mister general,
listen to me, mister general,
I am also a valiant man.
I want you to shoot me,
I want you to shoot me
in public before the people."

Adiós, reloj de Durango,	Good-bye, clock of Durango,
adiós, reloj de Durango,	good-bye, clock of Durango,
sus horas me atormentaban.	your hours tormented me.
Solito a mí maldiciendo,	Cursing me alone,
solito a mí maldiciendo	cursing me alone,
las horas que me faltaban.	the hours I had left.
Ya con esta me despido,	With this I bid you farewell,
ya con esta me despido,	with this I bid you farewell,
porque cantar ya no puedo.	because I can't sing any longer.
Señores, son las mañanas,	Señores, this is the ballad,
señores, son las mañanas	señores, this is the ballad
de Benjamín Argumedo.	of Benjamín Argumedo.

One of the greatest *corridistas* of his time is Roberto Martínez of Albuquerque, New Mexico, who performs with Los Reyes de Albuquerque. Roberto Martínez has composed many *corridos,* one of the best known of which is *El corrido de Río Arriba*. This celebrated ballad tells the story of the 1967 raid on the courthouse in Tierra Amarilla, New Mexico, by the Alianza led by the Texas-born former preacher, Reyes López Tijerina. This was one of the most significant events during the twentieth century in Hispano New Mexico, in that it focused national attention on the ongoing controversy of Hispano land rights and the massive loss of common lands supposedly protected by the Treaty of Guadalupe Hidalgo of 1848.

Señor Martínez performed this *corrido* with his son, Lorenzo, on the violin and Ysidro Chávez on the *guitarrón*. Roberto Martínez sings and plays the *vihuela*. The two latter instruments are widely used in Mexico by *mariachis,* but until recently were seldom employed in the Río Grande del Norte by *músicos* who perform the traditional music of the north country. These musicians are professional and well known in the West among Spanish-speaking people.

El corrido de Río Arriba reflects the tradition of journalism within *corrido* form. Martínez wrote it within hours of hearing news of the events and sang it on an Albuquerque radio station a few days later. He reports the momentous events much more objectively than any of the newspapers of New Mexico at the time.

El corrido de Río Arriba

Written by Roberto Martínez
Performed by Roberto and Lorenzo Martínez
and Ysidro Chávez

El corrido de Río Arriba

Roberto Martínez

Año de sesenta y siete
cinco de junio fue el día,
hubo una revolución
allá por Tierra Amarilla.

Allá en la casa de corte,
pueblo de Tierra Amarilla,
Nuevo México el estado,
Condado de Río Arriba.

Un grupo de nuestra raza
muy descontentos bajaron.
Y en oficiales de estado
su venganza ellos tomaron.

Su jefe les suplicaba:
"No debería haber violencia."
Pero no los controlaba,
pues perdieron la paciencia.

Un diputado en el suelo
se queja con agonía,
con una bala en el pecho,
allá por Tierra Amarilla.

Corrido de Río Arriba

Roberto Martínez

In the year of sixty-seven
the fifth of June was the day,
there was a revolution
up there in Tierra Amarilla.

There at the court house,
town of Tierra Amarilla,
New Mexico the state,
Río Arriba the county.

A group of our people
came down very discontented.
And on state officials
they took vengeance.

Their leader begged them:
"There should be no violence."
But he didn't control them
Well, they lost their patience

A deputy on the floor
moans in agony,
with a bullet in his chest,
up there in Tierra Amarilla.

Las mujeres y los niños
iban corriendo y llorando.
En ese instante pensamos
que el mundo se iba acabando.

Fueron treinta que lograron
para la sierra escapar.
Y el gobernador llamó
a la Guardia Nacional.

Cuando fueron capturados
a la prisión los llevaron,
para que fueran juzgados
del crimen que se acusaron.

Este corrido termina
cuando se haga la justicia,
para que no se repita
lo de allá en Tierra Amarilla.

The women and children
went running and crying.
At that moment we thought
that the world was ending.

There were thirty that managed
to escape to the mountains.
And the governor called up
the National Guard.

When they were captured
they took them to prison,
so they would be judged
for the crime of which they were accused.

This corrido will end
when justice is done,
so that what happened in Tierra Amarilla
will not be repeated.

Albino Gómez,
Las Tablas, New Mexico.

*(Except where otherwise noted, all
photographs are by Jack Parsons.)*

Abenicio Montoya and Benny Bustos, Santa Fe, New Mexico.

José Jaramillo,
Albuquerque,
New Mexico

Virginia Bernal,
Ratón, New Mexico

Archie and María Garduño,
Las Vegas, New Mexico

Geraldo José Martínez,
Las Vegas, New Mexico

Julia Jaramillo and Ernesto Montoya, Taos, New Mexico

José Archuleta and Pablo Trujillo, Taos, New Mexico

Floyd Trujillo, Abiquiú, New Mexico

Roberto Mondragón,
Cuyamungué, New Mexico

Sam Armijo,
Gladstone, New Mexico

Mrs. Guadalupe Urioste, Las Vegas, New Mexico

Abade Martínez,
San Luis, Colorado

Santiago Martínez,
Las Vegas, New Mexico

71

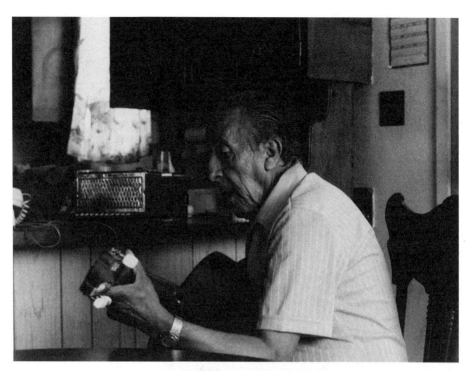

José Domingo Romero,
Las Vegas, New Mexico
Photo by Jack Loeffler

Ernesto Montoya,
Taos, New Mexico
Photo by Jack Loeffler

Margaret Saavedra,
Albuquerque, New
Mexico

Luis Martínez,
Ratón, New Mexico

Edwin Berry,
Tomé, New Mexico

Pete, Chris, and
Manuel Chávez,
Española, New Mexico

Carmen Araiza,
La Mesa, New Mexico

Ciprianito and
Cipriano Vigil,
El Rito, New Mexico

Rumaldo Guilez and
Concepción "Chon"
Guilez, Tularosa, New
Mexico

Claudio Sáenz,
La Mesa, New Mexico

Lorenzo and Roberto Martínez, Albuquerque, New Mexico

William Pacheco, Señora y Señor Pete Casías, Romeroville, Colorado
Photo by Jack Loeffler.

Edulia Romero,
Alamosa, Colorado

Juan De La O and Vivián De La O,
Albuquerque, New Mexico

Manuel Rosas and Roger Gabaldón,
Socorro, New Mexico

Vicente Montoya, Margarito Olivas, and Juanita Olivas,
Las Vegas, New Mexico

Felix Vega and Pete Maese,
Las Cruces, New Mexico

Solomón Chávez,
Alamosa, Colorado

Cleofes Ortiz and
Augustine Chávez,
Ribera, New Mexico

Toney Sánchez,
Clayton, New Mexico

Max and Antonia Apodaca,
Rociada, New Mexico

Julián Contreras,
Leasburg, New Mexico

Pepe Hidalgo,
Tommy Delgadillo,
and Bernie Romero,
Lemitar, New Mexico

Johnny Flórez
and Raúl García,
Las Cruces,
New Mexico

Enrique Yara,
Watrous,
New Mexico

Ventura Rael,
Las Cruces,
New Mexico

CHAPTER FOUR

Canciones

In *Spanish Folk Poetry of New Mexico,* Arthur L. Campa gave an excellent description of the literary aspects of the musical form known as the *canción.* He included the texts of fifty *canciones* that enjoyed popularity in New Mexico at the time of publication (1946). In the intervening decades many of these *canciones* have faded from the collective memory of *la gente*; however, *canciones* such as *Cielito lindo* and *El rancho grande* have exploded into American popular culture and have almost become clichés, in the sense that many non-Hispanos associate these songs and a few others with the Spanish-speaking people of North America.

The *canción* enjoys a freedom of form not available in the *corridos, romances, inditas,* and *décimas.* According to Campa,

> A *canción* may appear in any verse form that strikes the composer's fancy, and, while the theme may be lyrical for the most part, there is a wide range of subjects that may be treated.
>
> The subjective quality of the *canción* reveals more readily the fine nuances of folk sensibility in outpourings of the lovelorn, in candid denunciations of unrequited lovers, in sincere expressions of undying affection, and in melancholy murmurings of the introvert.

The *canción* is largely concerned with love, but as Robb mentions, themes of mourning, happiness, boasting, and specific localities are found among these songs. The *canción* affords those with a penchant for classification the opportunity to disagree. For example Mendoza regards the song *El Quelite* as a *corrido* eulogizing a city. Jesús Romero Flores considers the same song a *corrido de la revolución,* to which he assigns the date 1929. Robb has classified *El Quelite* as a *canción* expressing "love's longing."

The word *quelite* means "lamb's quarters" (an edible plant) in both New and old Mexico. About fifty kilometers north of Mazatlán, Sinaloa, is the town of El Quelite, an area of Mexico that is verdant and dreamy, a perfect setting for lovers. El Quelite lies nears the western foothills of the Sierra Madre Occidental, about 170 kilometers southwest of the city of Durango, an area that suffered great disruption during *la revolución.* Taking all of this into account, it seems that everyone has a plausible reason for each of the classifications.

It is interesting to note that we have recorded versions of *El Quelite* in La Mesa, Las Vegas, and Ratón, New Mexico, as well as in Conejos, Colorado, which indicates some sense of its popularity.

It is true that *canciones* elicit an array of emotional fibrillations. Undoubtedly many *canciones* have been composed professionally for popular consumption and have subsequently been absorbed into the folk tradition. Ethnomusicologist James Leger has stated his opinion that folk music is whatever is regarded to be folk music by the people, regardless of origin.

A significant proportion of the vocal music in our collection of Hispano folk songs may be regarded as *canciones*. In addition there are many instrumental versions of *canciones*. We have noted that among *la gente* of the region, the word *canción* means "song"–any song. Campa mentioned this much earlier in this century, regarding the word as a "generic name that has always been used in New Mexico to include *décimas, corridos, cuandos* and *inditas* …"

All but two of the *canciones* included here are reputed to be of Mexican provenance. Earlier in the century, Campa noted several *canciones* that originated in New Mexico. He also listed nine from Spain that were popular in New Mexico and southern Colorado. To date we have encountered none of these in our field recording. Robb lists ninety-three *canciones* in his work, many of which appear in our collection.

A *canción* entitled *El nuevo Don Simón* was noted by Campa to have appeared in a collection of Mexican *canciones* in 1888. It is conceivable that a version entitled *Don Simón de mi vida* appeared on the Mexican scene even earlier. Robb notes a complete version of *Don Simón* that was published in the November 2, 1895, edition of *El Independiente* in Las Vegas, New Mexico. Several different versions of this *canción* have been popular regionally for nearly a century. We have recorded four versions as well as another concerning the wife of Don Simón. Mysteriously no one seems to know who Don Simón really was. He may have been a character who entertained audiences between acts in Mexico City music halls. Whoever he was, he is now immortalized as a man of great patience who complains of change and the shocking conduct of the younger generation. It is interesting that bemoaning the alleged shortcomings of young people has become a tradition in its own right, and one not restricted to Hispano culture.

The version of *Don Simón de mi vida* presented here was sung by Señora Lucy Jaramillo of Conejos, Colorado. She accompanied herself on the twelve-string guitar. This recording was made in her home in the summer of 1980.

Don Simón de mi vida

Performed by Lucy Jaramillo

Don Simón de mi vida

Lucy Jaramillo

Don Simón, don Simón de mi vida,
en los años que me dió el Señor,
nunca he visto lo que ahora he mirado.
¡Ay, qué tiempos, señor don Simón!

En mis tiempos las niñas usaban
sus rosarios en la procesión,
y sus ojos mostraban humildes.
¡Ay, qué tiempos, señor don Simón!

Ahora, casi les salen los dientes
cuando escriben cartitas de amor,
y cuando sus padres les hablan, se ríen.
¡Ay, qué tiempos, señor don Simón!

En mis tiempos las niñas usaban
por adorno un gran peinetón
y sus túnicos de medio paso.
¡Ay, qué tiempos, señor don Simón!

Hoy las vemos que parecen ratas
y en las frentes colas de ratón,
¡tanto polvo se dan que parecen
panaderas, señor don Simón!

Don Simón of My Life

Lucy Jaramillo

Don Simón, Don Simón my dear friend,
in the years that the Lord gave me,
never have I seen what I am seeing now.
Oh, what times, Señor Don Simón!

In my day the young women used
their rosaries in the procession,
and they showed humility in their eyes.
Oh, what times, Señor Don Simón!

Now, they almost bare their teeth
when they write their little love letters,
and when parents talk to them they laugh.
Oh, what times, Señor Don Simón!

In my day the young women used
as adornment a big comb
and their midlength dresses.
Oh, what times, Señor Don Simón!

Today we see they look like rats
and on their foreheads rat tails,
with so much powder on they look like
bakers, Señor Don Simón!

*T*ecolote de guadaña is an old *canción* that apparently originated in Mexico. John Robb cites seven *canciones* involving *tecolotes*, or owls, one of which mentions Santa Anna, the nineteenth-century Mexican general who led forces against Spain, the United States, and the Emperor Maximilian. In that version, as in many others, the *tecolote* is actually a young man. Edwin Berry, the master singer from Tomé, New Mexico, calls the owl in his version a "personification." In all these versions the *tecolote* personifies a young man daydreaming. In the case of *Tecolote de guadaña,* the young man expresses his envy for the wings of an owl that he might fly off to visit his beloved.

In many Indian cultures, the owl is a harbinger of death. In the Jameson collection of Hispano legends of New Mexico, at least twenty-eight instances of witches becoming owls are cited. Apparently, *tecolote* referred to young soldiers who were bachelors in Mexico in the nineteenth century, just as "dogfaces" referred to American infantrymen during World War II. Bearing this in mind, it is easy to visualize a young Mexican soldier on guard duty imagining himself flying away from war into his lover's arms.

In this version of *Tecolote de guadaña*, a *despedida* set to a *huapango* occurs that seems strangely out of context. It has been suggested that this *huapango* was not actually part of the original *canción* but was added later. This version was sung by Julia Jaramillo accompanied by the late Ernesto Montoya, both of Taos, New Mexico. This is the same version included in the film *La música de los viejos*.

Tecolote de guadaña

Julia Jaramillo

Tecolote de guadaña,
pájaro madrugador,
tecolote de guadaña,
pájaro madrugador,
quién tuviera tus alitas,
quién tuviera tus alitas,
quién tuviera tus alitas,
para ir a ver a mi amor,
para ir a ver a mi amor.
coro:
Ti curi, curi, curi, cu,
ti curi, curi, curi, cu,
ti curi, curi, curi, cu,
pobrecito tecolote,
ya se cansa de llorar.

Si yo fuera tecolote
no me ocuparía en volar,
si yo fuera tecolote,
no me ocuparía en volar.
Me quedaría en mi nidito,
me quedaría en mi nidito,
me quedaría en mi nidito,
acabándome de criar,
acabándome de criar.

coro

¿Tecolote, qué haces ahí,
sentado en esa pared?
¿Tecolote, qué haces ahí,
sentado en esa pared?
Esperando a su tecolota,
esperando a su tecolota,
esperando a su tecolota,
que le traiga que comer,
que le traiga que comer.

coro

Owl in the Hayloft

Julia Jaramillo

Owl in the hayloft,
early rising bird,
owl in the hayloft,
early rising bird,
if only I had your little wings,
if only I had your little wings,
if only I had your little wings,
to go and see my love,
to go and see my love.
chorus:
Ti curi, curi, curi, cu,
ti curi, curi, curi, cu,
ti curi, curi, curi, cu,
the poor little owl,
is already tired of crying.

If I were an owl,
I wouldn't worry about flying,
if I were an owl,
I wouldn't worry about flying.
I would remain in my little nest,
I would remain in my little nest,
I would remain in my little nest,
and finish growing,
and finish growing.

chorus

Little owl, what are you doing there
perched upon that wall,
little owl, what are you doing there
perched upon that wall?
Waiting for his love,
waiting for his love,
waiting for his love,
to bring him something to eat,
to bring him something to eat.

chorus

Tecolote de guadaña

Performed by Julia Jaramillo y Ernesto Montoya

Si yo fuera tecolote	If I were an owl,
no me ocuparía en volar,	I wouldn't worry about flying,
si yo fuera tecolote,	if I were an owl,
no me ocuparía en volar.	I wouldn't worry about flying.
Me quedaría en mi nidito,	I would remain in my little nest,
me quedaría en mi nidito,	I would remain in my little nest,
me quedaría en mi nidito,	I would remain in my little nest,
acabándome de criar,	and finish growing,
acabándome de criar.	and finish growing.
coro	*chorus*
Ya el carretero se va,	Now the wagon master is leaving,
ya se va para Durango.	he is going to Durango.
Ya el carretero no va	But now he is not going
porque le falta ese chango.	because his monkey is missing.
¡Señor carretero, le vengo a avisar	Mr. Wagon master, I come to warn you
que sus animales se le van a ahogar,	that your animals are going to drown,
unos en la arena y otros en el mar,	some in the sand, others in the sea,
Señor carretero, le vengo a avisar!	Mr. Wagon master, I come to warn you.

One of the most poignant *canciones* we have ever recorded is entitled *La huerfanita*, "The little orphan girl." It recalls the *décima*, *El huérfano*, mentioned in a later chapter. *La gente* have a deep concern for family, and those who are orphaned are regarded to have suffered one of life's greatest misfortunes. Candelaria Torres of Costilla, New Mexico, is held in high esteem as a *música* and as a *bailadora*. She learned this *canción* from Andrew Jacobs in Amalia, New Mexico, in 1930. Her sons, Andy and Dennis Torres, performed the guitar accompaniment.

La huerfanita	**The Little Orphan Girl**
Candelaria Torres	Candelaria Torres
Allá en la cima	There at the summit
de una montaña,	of a mountain,
tristes cabañas	the sad cabins
donde nací.	where I was born.
Andando un día	Walking one day
en la cazada,	while hunting,
una joven bella	a beautiful young girl
yo conocí.	I met.
Luego al momento	Then in a moment
me dirigí,	I went to where
donde ella estaba	she was
y la saludé.	and greeted her.

La Huerfanita

Performed by Candelaria, Andy y Dennis Torres

Ella muy triste
con ojos bajos,
me dio su mano
y se la estreché.

She very sad
with lowered eyes,
gave me her hand
and I squeezed it.

Yo le hice varias
observaciones,
y ella muy triste
las escuchó.

I made various
remarks,
and she very sad
listened to them.

Le pregunté
si tendría sus padres,
y ella llorando
me dijo "no."

I asked her
if she had her parents,
and she crying
told me "no."

"Por mis desdichas
soy huerfanita,
fui abandonada
yo en mi niñez.

"By my misfortune
I am an orphan,
I was abandoned
in my childhood.

Yo no recuerdo
estaría muy chica,
tendría la edad
que sería un mes.

I don't remember
I must have been very small,
I would have been the
age of one month.

Pasaron días
pasaron años,
una familia
honrada me crió.

Days passed
years passed,
and an honorable family
raised me.

Por ellos mismos
vine sabiendo,
lo que a mis padres
les sucedió.

Through them
I came to know,
what happened
to my parents.

Pasaron días
pasaron años,
un sentimiento
me hizo llorar.

Salí a los campos
buscando alivio,
buscando alivio
sobre el pesar."

"Si quieres, niña,
venir conmigo,
aquí a la choza
donde nací.

Allí estaremos
los dos juntitos,
sin separarnos
hasta el morir."

Allá en la casa
donde la criaron,
allí logré
la oportunidad.

Yo les pedí
la mano de ella,
y ellos me dieron
su voluntad.

Pues nos casamos
y se acabaron,
las penas mías
y de ella también.

Desde el día
que nos casamos,
no hemos tenido
ningún desdén.

Aquí se acaban
amigos míos,
los tristes versos
de un cazador.

Estos versitos
fueron compuestos
por él que sufre
y sabe de amor.

Days passed
years passed,
a feeling
made me cry.

I went out into the country
looking for relief,
looking for relief
from my suffering."

"If you want, girl,
come with me,
here to the house
where I was born.

There we will be
both together,
without separating
until death."

There in the house
where they raised her,
there I had
my opportunity.

I asked them
for her hand,
and they told me
their wishes.

Well, we got married
and all my pain
ended and
hers, too.

From the day
that we were married
we haven't had
any conflict.

Here, my friends,
come to an end
the sad verses
of a hunter.

These little verses
were composed
by he that suffers
and knows of love.

Four versions of *Feria de las flores* appear in our archive of recordings. This is a *canción* with a beautiful, expressive melody. We have included an instrumental version to demonstrate an unusual piano rendition of folk music.

This version of *Feria de las flores* was performed by Señora Margaret Saavedra of Albuquerque, New Mexico. Señora Saavedra learned to play the piano when she was a young girl living in Albuquerque's Old Town. This recording was made in her home in 1980, when Señora Saavedra was eighty-three years old.

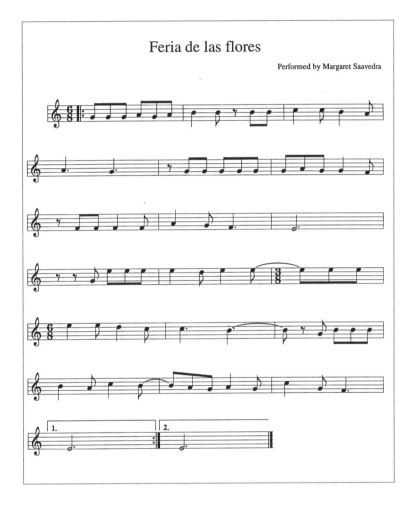

When Julia Jaramillo was six years old, an orphaned lad from Tampico, Tamaulipas, Mexico, found his way north to Taos, New Mexico, where he went to work for Señora Jaramillo's father. The boy's name was José Peña, and he sang a very strange *canción* that Señora Jaramillo subsequently found in an old *cancionero* that had been used by her mother. The *canción* is entitled *La boda negra*, and it recounts the tragic tale of a young man whose betrothed died. After many frustrating nights of visiting her grave, the young man returned to the camposanto for the last time and exhumed the skeletal remains of his sweetheart. He celebrated *la boda negra*, the black wedding, made love to her, and fell asleep forever. This *canción* is given an extra sense of eeriness in that it is recounted by a grave digger.

The version of *La boda negra* presented here was recorded in the home of Ernesto Montoya, who accompanied Señora Jaramillo as she sang.

La boda negra

Julia Jaramillo

Oye la historia que contó un día,
el viejo enterrador de la comarca.
Era un amante que por suerte impía
su dulce bien le arrebató la parca.

Todas las noches iba al cementerio
a visitar la tumba de la hermosa.
La gente murmuraba con misterio,
¡es un muerto escapado de la fosa!

En una noche horrenda hizo pedazos
el mármol de la tumba abandonada.
Cavó la tierra y llevó en sus brazos
el rígido esqueleto de su amada.

Black Wedding

Julia Jaramillo

Listen to the story that was told one day
by the old gravedigger of the region.
There was once a lover who by impious luck
had his sweet love snatched away by death.

Every night he went to the cemetery
to visit the grave of the beautiful woman.
The people would murmur with mystery,
He's a corpse escaped from the grave!

One horrible night he smashed
the marble of the abandoned tomb.
He dug in the earth and carried in his arms
the rigid skeleton of his beloved.

La boda negra

Performed by Julia Jaramillo y Ernesto Montoya

Y allá en la triste habitación sombría
de un cirio fúnebre de llama incierta,
sentó a su lado la osamenta fría
y celebró las bodas con la muerta.

Ató con cintas los desnudos huesos,
el yerto cráneo coronó de flores.
La horrible boca le cubrió de besos
y le contó sonriendo sus amores.

Llevó la novia al tálamo mullido,
se acostó junto a ella enamorado
y para siempre se quedó dormido
el esqueleto rígido abrazado.

Oye la historia que contó un día,
el viejo enterrador de la comarca.
Era un amante que por suerte impía
su dulce bien le arrebató la parca.

And there in his sad shadowy room
by the funereal flicker of candlelight,
he sat the cold skeleton by his side
and celebrated marriage with her.

He tied her fleshless bones with ribbons
and crowned the stiff skull with flowers.
He covered the horrible mouth with kisses,
and smiling, told her of his love.

He carried his bride to the downy bridal bed
and lay down with her, enamored,
and he remained asleep forever,
embracing the rigid skeleton.

Listen to the story that was told one day
by the old gravedigger of the region.
There was once a lover who by impious luck
had his sweet love snatched away by death.

*L*upita divina is an old *canción* that Edwin Berry said his mother regarded as a diplomatic song. Perhaps the "flower of Nicaragua" was related to someone in the political hierarchy. It is certainly a love song filled with tender phrases that exude the essence of sentimentality associated with the lovelorn.

Lupita divina contains one of the *coplas,* or couplets, commonly heard in *Las mañanitas,* the Spanish ceremonial birthday song. Aurelio Espinosa has made note of the free-floating nature of the *copla,* an independent quatrain that is recited or sung as it skips from *canción* to *canción.*

The version of *Lupita divina* included here was recorded in the home of Edwin Berry in Tomé, New Mexico. According to Arthur Campa the later *versos* of *Lupita divina* were included in the Mexican *canción* entitled *La despedida,* which was written by Ruperto J. Aldana in Lagos de Moreno, Jalisco, Mexico.

Lupita divina

Performed by Edwin Berry

Lupita divina

Edwin Berry

Eres Lupita divina
como los rayos del sol.
Eres la flor de Nicaragua,
dueña de mi corazón.

Recibe pues, esta canción.
Eres Lupita divina
como los rayos del sol.

El día en que tú naciste
nacieron todas las flores,
y en la pila del bautismo
cantaron los ruiseñores.

Recibe pues, esta canción.
Eres Lupita divina
como los rayos del sol.

Eres la flor de Nicaragua
dueña de mi corazón.
Recibe pues, esta canción.

Divine Lupita

Edwin Berry

You are divine Lupita
like the rays of the sun.
You are the flower of Nicaragua,
the keeper of my heart.

Receive then, this song.
You are divine Lupita,
like the rays of the sun.

On the day you were born
all the flowers were born,
and at the baptismal font
all the nightingales sang.

Receive then, this song.
You are divine Lupita
like the rays of the sun.

You are the flower of Nicaragua
the keeper of my heart.
Receive then, this song.

L*a mancornadora* is a *canción* that deals with betrayal in love. The word *mancornadora* refers to a two-timing woman, according to Rubén Cobos in his *Dictionary of New Mexico and Southern Colorado Spanish*. The six versions we have recorded were performed in Conejos, Colorado, and Taos, Las Vegas, and Tomé, New Mexico. The version presented in Robb's work was recorded in Cuba, New Mexico, in 1944.

The version of *La mancornadora* included here was performed by María and Archie Garduño of Las Vegas, New Mexico. María Garduño is the niece of José Domingo Romero of Las Vegas, whose music is also included in this work. In this version, María plays the guitar and Archie plays the *requinto*.

La mancornadora

María & Archie Garduño

Ando ausente del bien que adoré,
apasionado por una mujer.
Sólo cantando disipo mis penas
con las copas llenas voy a divagar.

Two-Timing Woman

María & Archie Garduño

I wander absent from the one I loved,
filled with passion for another woman.
Now only singing can dissolve my pain,
with my cups full will I wander.

Si lo hicistes de mala intención
o con el fin de hacerme padecer,
tú bien sabes que vivo entre flores
y nuevos amores me deben querer.

Si tú fueras legal con mi amor,
tú gozarías de mi protección,
pero en el mundo tú fuistes traidora,
la mancornadora de mi corazón.

La despedida yo no se las doy,
la despedida será una canción,
la despedida yo se las daré
cuando yo me vaya de esta población.

If you did it with bad intentions
or for the purpose of making me suffer,
you know well that I live among flowers
and new loves will surely desire me.

If you were faithful with my love,
you would enjoy my protection,
but in this world you were a traitress,
the two-timer of my heart.

My farewell I will not bid you,
my farewell will be a song,
I will only bid farewell
when I leave this town.

La mancornadora

Performed by María y Archie Garduño

El Quelite is one of the most famous love songs of the Mexican Revolution. Although *quelites* are the beloved wild "lambs quarter" greens eaten by people living off the land, in this song it refers to a community near the Río Presidio in the state of Sinaloa. The sense of nostalgia and longing in the lyrics reflects the massive social displacement that the Mexican people suffered in their civil war.

One of the best known and most beloved of the musicians in southern New Mexico is Carmen Araiza of La Mesa, which is just a few miles north of the current international boundary with Mexico. Señora Araiza has performed with many musicians on both sides of the border. She plays both the guitar and the mandolin. The version of *El Quelite* included here was presented in the film *La música de los viejos*.

El Quelite

Carmen Araiza

¡Qué bonito es el Quelite,
bien haya quién lo formó,
que por sus orillas tiene
de quién acordarme yo!

Al pie de un limón muy verde
me dió sueño y me dormí,
y me despertó un gallito
diciendo "quiquiriquí."

Camino de San Ignacio,
camino de San Andrés,
no dejes amor pendiente
como el que dejaste ayer.

Mañana me voy, mañana,
mañana me voy de aquí,
el consuelo que me queda
que se han de acordar de mí.

Yo no canto porque sé,
ni porque mi voz sea buena,
canto porque soy alegre
en mí tierra y en la ajena.

¡Qué bonito es el Quelite,
bien haya quién lo formó,
que por sus orillas tiene
de quién acordarme yo!

Quelite

Carmen Araiza

How beautiful is Quelite,
blessed was he who formed it,
for along its outskirts there is
someone I will remember!

At the foot of a very green lemon tree
I became drowsy and fell asleep
and was awakened by a little rooster
crying "ki ki ri ki."

Road of San Ignacio,
road of San Andrés,
do not leave love waiting
like the one you left yesterday.

Tomorrow I am going, tomorrow,
tomorrow I am leaving here,
my only consolation is
that they are bound to remember me.

I do not sing because I know how to,
nor because my voice is good,
I sing because I am happy
in my land and in faraway lands.

How beautiful is Quelite,
blessed was he who formed it,
for along its outskirts there is
someone I will remember!

El Quelite

Performed by Carmen Araiza

C anción mixteca was composed by José López Alvarez before 1934. It is one of those songs that enjoyed great popularity in Mexico and subsequently came northward to be accepted into the folk tradition of New Mexico and southern Colorado. María Garduño of Las Vegas regards this as a *canción* for those who are far from home and who long for their native land. Edwin Berry of Tomé, New Mexico, said that this song frequently appears in soundtracks for Spanish language films. It is definitely a classic example of the *canción* form. Lamadrid notes here that the singers will sometimes use different words in the same verse. Without any compromise of poetic unity, here *cielo,* or sky, is substituted for *suelo,* or land, the word that usually appears in this well-known verse. This kind of license is typical in oral transmission and accounts for the many variations of traditional and popular songs.

One of the most spirited of the five versions of *Canción mixteca* we have recorded was performed by Socorro Trio members Bernie Romero, Tommy Delgadillo, and Pepe Hidalgo, who live in the vicinity of Socorro, New Mexico. This was recorded in a restaurant as the *músicos* performed for the clientele.

Canción mixteca	Mixtec Song
Socorro Trío	Socorro Trio
¡Qué lejos estoy del cielo	How far away I am from the skies
donde he nacido,	where I was born
y más queda atarse al viento	and I can only tie my thoughts
mi pensamiento,	to the wind.
y al verme tan solo y triste	And seeing myself so alone and sad
cuál hoja al viento,	like a leaf blowing in the wind,
quisiera llorar,	I feel like crying,
quisiera morir	I feel like dying
de sentimiento!	of nostalgia!
¡O, tierra del sol,	Oh, land of the sun,
suspiro por verte,	I sigh to see you
y ahora que lejos me encuentro	and now I'm so far away,
sin luz, sin amor,	without light, without love,
y al verme tan solo y triste,	and on seeing myself so alone and sad,
cuál hoja al viento,	like a leaf blowing in the wind,
quisiera llorar,	I feel like crying,
quisiera morir	I feel like dying
de sentimiento!	of nostalgia!
¡Qué lejos estoy del suelo	How far away I am from the land
donde he nacido,	where I was born,
inmensa nostalgia invade	an immense nostalgia
mi pensamiento,	invades my thoughts,
y al verme tan solo y triste,	and on seeing myself so alone and sad,
cuál hoja al viento,	like a leaf blowing in the wind,
quisiera llorar,	I feel like crying,
quisiera morir	I feel like dying
de sentimiento!	of nostalgia!

Canción Mixteca

Performed by Bernie Romero, Pepe Hidalgo y Tommy Delgadillo

(Continued on next page)

Of Capullito de alelí Edwin Berry recalls Juan De La O singing this song over radio station KGGM in Albuquerque from 1929 to 1942. The radio announcer at that time was Enrique Tafoya. Señor Berry defines the *capullo* as the husk that covers the beautiful lily flower, *alelí*. The version presented here was performed on the accordion by José Jaramillo at his home in Albuquerque. At the time of recording, Señor Jaramillo was sixty-eight years old.

Capullito de alelí

Performed by José Jaramillo

Many years ago when he worked as a *vaquero*, or cowboy, Emilio Ortiz wrote a wonderful *canción* depicting his lifestyle. To any who have lived close to the land in New Mexico, *Canción del vaquero* elicits a poignant tickling of the funny bone. This presentation of his own *canción* was made by Emilio Ortiz in his home in Socorro, New Mexico. He was nearly sixty-eight years old at the time of recording.

Canción del vaquero

Emilio Ortiz

Esta es la vida
que pasa un vaquero,
que para amasar
usa su sombrero.

De charola tiene
un pedazo de cuero
para echar sus galletas
entre el cenicero.

¡Qué triste se me hacen
las horas del día,
más alegre estoy
cuando echo tortillas!

Unas salen crudas,
otras bien cocidas,
unas salen negras
y otras torcidas.

Yo tenía mi puela
en un rincón colgada,
porque los ratones
la usan de guitarra.

No cabe ni duda
que bailen con ella,
porque entre la harina
les hallo su huella.

También los vecinos
que son los coyotes,
¡qué bonitas piezas
cantan en las noches!

Cowboy Song

Emilio Ortiz

This is the life
that a cowboy leads,
to knead dough
he uses his hat.

As a bowl he has
a piece of leather,
to make his biscuits
in the ashes of the fire.

How sad the hours
of the day seem to me,
I am much happier
when I'm making tortillas!

Some turn out raw,
others well cooked,
some come out black,
and others warped.

I have my skillet
hung up in a corner
because the mice
use it as a guitar.

There is no doubt
they dance with it
because in the flour
I find their tracks.

Also, the neighbors
who are coyotes,
what beautiful pieces
they sing at night!

Bailan cuadrillas,
y polkas y chotes,
también los zorrillos
valsean al trote.

Y cuando me acuesto,
rendido y cansado,
debajo mi almohada
yo voy a estar cantando.

Las víboras pasan
casi golpeando,
debajo mi almohada
forman su fandango.

They dance quadrilles,
polkas and schottisches,
the skunks also
waltz the fox trot.

And when I lie down,
worn out and tired,
underneath my pillow
I'll be singing.

The snakes pass
almost striking me,
underneath my pillow
they dance their fandango.

Canción del vaquero

Performed by Emilio Ortiz

La Llorona is one of the most haunting and beautiful songs ever to have emerged in the Western Hemisphere. Some attribute its composition to Tata Nacho, while others regard it as having been written by an anonymous *músico*. It seems to have appeared sometime around 1930. Because of its lyrical quality, I consider it to be a *canción*. Ethnomusicologist Brenda Romero concurs but with the qualification that it is also considered to be a *vals oaxaqueño,* or waltz from Oaxaca.

The legend of *La Llorona* is ubiquitous in Mesoamerica, ranging northward from Oaxaca, Mexico, to the Río Grande del Norte. The legend itself is ancient, while the melody is thought by some to have originated in Mexico in the mid-nineteenth century. The melody suggests an Andalusian influence.

While María and the Virgin of Guadalupe represent all that is light, good, and spiritually evolved, *La Llorona*, the weeping woman, presents the darker aspect of the feminine principle. She is conceived to be an *ánima en pena,* or suffering soul, the woeful ghost of a woman who drowned her children and now wanders endlessly searching for them. Her wails in the night are a harbinger of death. In one aspect she is an Aztec goddess, while in another she is regarded as the shade of Malinche, the Indian woman who abandoned her people to become the paramour of and interpreter for Hernán Cortez. Her path winds through many legends and levels of meaning. She taps the chthonic depths of the Hispano psyche. With her great beauty and tragic air, she is of great danger to the Hispano male, who is particularly susceptible to her presence. *La Llorona* is an archetypal figure with many facets and functions.

In the lyrics the singer identifies himself as *"el Negro."* Enrique R. Lamadrid has pointed out that this was the nickname of a famous troubadour of bygone days. *Negro* means "black" in Spanish but is a widely used term of endearment, regardless of the race of the person referred to.

Cipriano Vigil, whose family photograph appears on the front cover of this book, is regarded as one of the greatest Hispano folk musicians of the twentieth century. His elaborate arrangement of La Llorona is one of the trademarks of his repertoire.

La Llorona	**The Weeping Woman**
Cipriano Vigil	Cipriano Vigil
Todos me dicen el Negro, Llorona,	Everyone calls me "El Negro," Llorona,
negro pero cariñoso.	dark but affectionate.
Todos me dicen el Negro, Llorona,	Everyone calls me "El Negro," Llorona,
negro pero cariñoso.	dark but affectionate.
Yo soy como el chile verde, Llorona,	I am like the green chile, Llorona,
picante pero sabroso.	piquant but tasty.
Yo soy como el chile verde, Llorona,	I am like the green chile, Llorona,
picante pero sabroso.	hot but delicious.
Ay de mí, Llorona, Llorona!	Woe is me, Llorona!
Llorona de azul celeste.	Llorona of heavenly blue.
¡Ay de mí, Llorona, Llorona!	Woe is me, Llorona!
Llorona de azul celeste.	Llorona of heavenly blue.

Y aunque la vida me cueste, Llorona,
no dejaré de quererte.
Y aunque la vida me cueste, Llorona,
no dejaré de quererte.

Salías del templo un día Llorona,
Cuando al pasar yo te vi.
Salías del templo un día Llorona,
Cuando al pasar yo te vi.

Hermoso huipil llevabas Llorona,
que la Virgen te creí.
Hermoso huipil llevabas Llorona,
que la Virgen te creí.

Si al cielo subir pudiera, Llorona,
las estrellas te bajara.
Si al cielo subir pudiera, Llorona,
las estrellas te bajara.

La luna a tus pies pusiera, Llorona,
con el sol te coronará.
La luna a tus pies pusiera, Llorona,
con el sol te coronará.

And even though it cost me my life, Llorona,
I will never stop loving you.
And even though it cost me my life, Llorona,
I will never stop loving you.

You were leaving the temple one day, Llorona,
when I saw you pass by.
You were leaving the temple one day, Llorona,
when I saw you pass by.

Such a beautiful huipil you were wearing, Llorona,
that I thought you were the Virgin (Mary).
Such a beautiful huipil you were wearing, Llorona,
that I thought you were the Virgin (Mary).

If I could climb up to the sky, Llorona,
I would bring down the stars for you.
If I could rise up to the sky, Llorona,
I would bring down the stars for you.

The moon I would put at your feet, Llorona,
and crown you with the sun.
The moon I would put at your feet, Llorona,
and crown you with the sun.

La Llorona

Performed by Cipiriano Vigil

A musical form that has only recently come into currency is the *nueva canción,* or "new song." As Enrique R. Lamadrid points out, this form was popularized in Chile during the time of Salvador Allende. Two *músicos* who both composed and performed *nueva canción* in its early days were Violeta Parra and Victor Jara. One of the first Chilean groups to perform in this musical medium was El Grupo Inti-Illimani. *Nueva canción* is now heard throughout the Americas, where it serves as the link between folk and more contemporary music as well as the social conscience of the hemisphere.

In New Mexico composer-performer Cipriano Vigil was introduced to *nueva canción* when he studied the traditional music of Mexico in the 1970s with the famed group Los Folkloristas. He has now composed numerous songs widely regarded as the *nueva canción* of New Mexico. Many of the younger *músicos* who have listened to Señor Vigil are currently accepting this genre as their own medium of musical expression in a time when survival of *Nuevo Mexicano* culture is regarded as threatened. It is fitting that a composition reflecting this new form be included in the present work.

Se ve triste el hombre conveys a deeply felt sentiment of *la gente* for the loss of the land after the American occupation. The common lands once shared by land grant communities are now in the hands of American ranchers, the Forest Service, and the Bureau of Land Management, all of them criticized at one time or another for their unwise use of the land. This *Nuevo Mexicano* protest song was written and performed by Cipriano Vigil. The melody is loosely transcribed.

Se ve triste el hombre

Cipriano Vigil

Entra el hombre cuartonero
a las entrañas de la sierra.
Sacan todos los pinos
y nos dejan sin madera,
sacan todos los pinos
y nos dejan sin madera.

Las montañas de mi tierra
en un tiempo de mi gente fueron.
Cuando entraron las Florestas
toditito recogieron,
cuando entraron las Florestas
toditito recogieron.

Se ve triste el hombre,
el hombre de la sierra.
Pues destrozaron la naturaleza,
le quitaron el agua y su tierra,
destrozaron la naturaleza,
le quitaron el agua y su tierra.

The Man Looks Sad

Cipriano Vigil

The logger enters
the heart of the mountains.
They take away all the pines
and leave us without any lumber,
they take away all the pines
and leave us without any lumber.

The mountains of my land
once belonged to my people.
When the Forest Service came
they claimed it all,
when the Forest Service came
they claimed it all.

The man looks sad,
the man from the mountains.
They destroyed Nature
and took away the water and the land,
they destroyed Nature
and took away the water and the land.

Se ve triste el hombre

Composed and performed by Cipriano Vigil

Hay que preservar lo nuestro.
Ya basta de "mi casa es suya."
No tenemos leña verde
ni para cocer tortillas,
no tenemos leña verde
ni para cocer tortillas.

Como si esto fuera todo,
todo lo que desahuciaron,
en el cuento de las tierras
las donaciones, ¿de quiénes fueron?
en el cuento de las tierras,
las donaciones, ¿de quiénes fueron?

Se ve triste el hombre,
el hombre de la sierra.
Pues destrozaron la naturaleza,
le quitaron el agua y su tierra,
destrozaron la naturaleza,
le quitaron el agua y su tierra.

En los tiempos de mi abuelo
cuando cercas no existían,
de esta piedra a aquel pinito
es la tierra mía,
de esta piedra a aquel pinito
es la tierra mía.

We must preserve what is ours.
Enough of, "my house is your house."
We don't even have green wood
to cook tortillas,
we don't even have green wood
to cook tortillas.

And as if that weren't enough,
everything that they did away with,
in the history of the land,
who else did the land grants belong to?
In the history of the land,
who else did the land grants belong to?

The man looks sad,
the man from the mountains.
They destroyed Nature
and took away the water and the land,
they destroyed Nature
and took away the water and the land.

In my grandfather's day,
when wire fences didn't exist,
from this rock to that little pine
my land extended,
from this rock to that little pine
my land extended.

Esos tiempos se acabaron,	Those days are gone,
nos quitaron toditito.	they have taken everything away.
Ahora nos miran y se ríen	Now they look at us and laugh
y nos ven como tontitos,	and see us as fools,
ahora nos miran y se ríen	now they look at us and laugh
y nos ven como tontitos.	and see us as fools.
Se ve triste el hombre,	The man looks sad,
el hombre de la sierra.	the man from the mountains.
Pues destrozaron la naturaleza,	They destroyed Nature
nos quitaron el agua y la tierra,	and took away the water and the land,
destrozaron la naturaleza,	they destroyed Nature
nos quitaron el agua y la tierra.	and took away the water and the land.

CHAPTER FIVE

La Música Ceremonial y Religiosa

L
AS MAÑANITAS BELONGS TO A TYPE OF commemorative *canción* sung throughout the Río Grande del Norte, especially to celebrate birthdays and inaugurations. *Mañanitas,* or dawn songs, have their roots in the tradition of French and Spanish troubadours, who often sang songs of love in the common language of the people. As dawn approached and a secret lover prepared to take his leave, he might sing a farewell song, which came to be known as a dawn song. Sometimes these *albas,* or *mañanitas,* were conversations between the troubadour and a friend posted outside to warn of danger; sometimes they were simply songs of departure. We have recorded six versions of this ceremonial song, all of which are beautifully expressive and convey the depth of regard *la gente* feel for their family and friends on birthdays and saints' days. One *música* mentioned that she calls an old and dear friend on her birthday every year and sings *Las mañanitas* to her over the telephone.

The version included here was performed by Señor Ventura Rael of Las Cruces, New Mexico, when he was seventy-nine years old.

Las mañanitas	**Morning Serenade**
Ventura Rael	Ventura Rael
¡Qué lindas son las mañanas cuando vengo a saludarte! Venimos todos con gusto, y a cesar hasta saludarte.	How beautiful are the mornings when I come to greet you. We all arrive with delight and cease all until we congratulate you.
Ya viene amaneciendo, ya la luz del día nos dio. Levántate de mañana, mira que amaneció.	Here comes the dawn now it gives us the light of day. Arise in the morning and see what has dawned.

Y el día que tú nacistes	On the day you were born
nacieron todas las flores,	all the flowers were born,
y en las pilas del bautismo	and at the baptismal fonts
cantaron los ruiseñores.	all the nightingales sang.
Ya viene amaneciendo,	Here comes the dawn
ya la luz del día nos dio.	now it gives us the light of day.
Levántate de mañana,	Arise in the morning
mira que amaneció.	and see what has dawned.

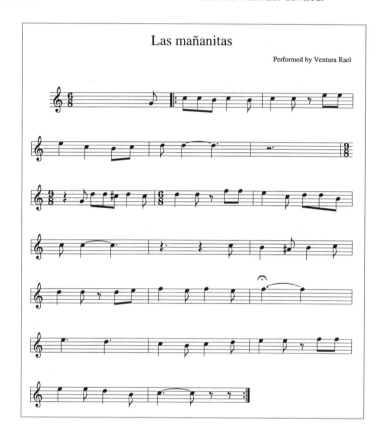

Los días del Año Nuevo, "days of the New Year," are sung on New Year's Eve and early New Year's morning in a custom called *dando los días,* or "giving the days." A wandering group of *músicos* and singers gathers outside the doors and windows of the homes of *la gente* throughout the villages, in much the same way that Christmas carolers sing at Christmas time. Lamadrid notes that the groups stop first at houses where someone is named Manuel, the patron saint of the New Year and one of the names of Jesus. After singing at the doorstop and waking up their neighbors, the *músicos* are invited inside to partake of food and drink, which sustain them against the deep wintry cold. After several *copitas* of *vino de capulín,* or chokecherry wine, and a few shots of whiskey, by the end of their wanderings their trails through the snow may seem ever more circuitous.

Some of these *versos* are improvised on the spot just as a good *entregador/a,* or singer of *entriegas,* composes as he or she sings at a wedding. The melody lines are similar to or identical with melody lines from the *Entriegas de los novios,* or "delivery of the newlyweds," so there is a strong traditional affiliation between the two forms. It is my opinion that *Los días del Año Nuevo* can be regarded as a form of *entriega,* or song of passage, from the old year into the new.

Los días del Año Nuevo are masterfully performed here by members of the Chávez family of Española, New Mexico. Pete Chávez has composed an impressive repertory of *versos* within the tradition he learned from an uncle. His brother, Manuel, accompanies him on the guitar, while his son, Chris, plays the violin. It is interesting to note that in their version, the melody line is in ABAB form, the violin playing the B line, the A line being sung. This gives the singer some respite through the long evening. Chris Chávez was ten years old at the time of this recording.

Los días del Año Nuevo

Para pisar esta casa,
pongo un pie, pongo los dos,
y a los dueños de esta casa
¡Buenos días les dé Dios!

Y aquí me paro en la puerta
yo les vine aquí a cantar,
a los mentados Manueles
pido permiso al lugar.

(¡que vivan!)

No quiero que se levanten
y que abandonen su cama,
solo les vengo a decir
"son las tres de la mañana."

Vayan a que se levanten
verán su patio regado,
con lágrimas de mis ojos
por allí la noche llorando.

Válgame Dios de los cielos
cómo se van los Manueles,
porque el Señor se llamaba
Manuelito de los Reyes.

Y escúchenme los Manueles
ya aquí caigo, aquí levanto,
es el día de Año Nuevo
el mero día de su santo.

Despierten ya los Manueles
de su sueño tan profundo,
y aquí a su casa ha llegado
la alegría de este mundo.

The Days of the New Year

To enter this house
I put one foot, then the other,
and to the owners of this house
May God give you a good day!

Here I stand in the doorway
I came here to sing,
and of the famous Manueles
I ask permission to be here.

(long may they live!)

I don't want them to get up
nor abandon their beds,
I've just come to say to them
"It's three in the morning!"

If you go and get up
you'll see your yard soaked
with tears from my eyes
and out there the night crying.

God of Heaven help me!
Look at these Manueles,
because Our Lord was named
Manuelito of the Kings.

Listen to me, you Manueles
I'm falling down, I'm getting up,
it is New Year's Day,
the day of your saint.

May the Manueles awake
from their profound sleep,
to their house has come
the happiness of this world.

Despierten ya de su sueño
asómense a su ventana,
llegamos al Año Nuevo
qué alegre está la mañana.

De mi casa he salido
con la nieve a la rodilla,
ya a la casa de los Manueles
a darles los buenos días.

Yo no canto porque sé
ni porque mi voz es buena,
yo canto pa' que no caiga
el penar sobre la ajena.

Ya mis amigos no gritan
y mi garganta ya no canta,
creo que ya necesitan
de esa agüita que ataranta.

Ya con esta me despido
rezando un Ave María,
que Dios te dé larga vida
por allí donde no había alegría.

May they wake up from their slumber
and go to their window,
we have come to the New Year
and the morning is joyful.

From my house I have come
with snow up to my knees,
to the house of the Manueles
to bring them this good morning.

I don't sing because I know how
nor because my voice is good,
I sing so that pain may not
fall upon the house of others.

My friends no longer cry out
and my throat no longer sings,
I think they need some of that
nice little water that makes you dizzy.

With this I take my leave
praying a Hail Mary,
may God give you long life
there where there was little joy.

Los días del Año Nuevo

Performed by Pete, Manuel y Chris Chávez

The other great holiday processional that involves neighbors singing in groups and visiting each other's houses is *Las Posadas,* or "the inns," which reenacts the Holy Family's trip to Bethlehem on the first Christmas. *Navidad,* the nativity feast of the *Santo Niño,* or Christ Child, brings hope and celebration into the community. In New Mexico as elsewhere, Christmas is a children's festival filled with memories, music, and feasting. As the *Noche Buena,* or Christmas Eve, approaches, the road to *Belén,* or Bethlehem, is shorter each night. The nine nights leading up to Christmas Eve are also observed with the musical processions of *Las Posadas,* in which the expectant parents of the Christ Child, San José y Santa María, come knocking at a different house each night, asking for lodging.

This version of *Las Posadas* is enacted yearly in the San José Barrio in Albuquerque by local parishioners. One group of musicians and singers is inside the house and the other outside. After the initial exchanges, the people inside the house recognize María and José and joyfully invite them inside, where a feast follows.

Las Posadas

Coro de San José

AFUERA:

En nombre del cielo os pido posada
pues no puede andar mi esposa amada.

ADENTRO:

Aquí no es mesón, sigan adelante
Yo no debo abrir no sea algún tunante.

AFUERA:

No seas inhumano, tennos caridad
que el Dios de los cielos te lo premiará.

ADENTRO:

Ya se pueden ir y no molestar
porque si me enfado os voy a apalear.

AFUERA:

Venimos rendidos desde Nazareth
Yo soy carpintero de nombre José.

ADENTRO:

No me importa el nombre, déjeme dormir
Pues que ya les digo que no hemos de abrir.

AFUERA:

Posada te pido amado casero
por sólo una noche la Reina del Cielo.

ADENTRO:

Pues si es una reina quien lo solicita
¿Cómo es que de noche anda tan solita?

The Inns

San José Choir

OUTSIDE:

In the name of heaven I ask you for lodging
well my beloved wife cannot walk.

INSIDE:

This is not an inn, keep going
I shouldn't open for it might be some rascal.

OUTSIDE:

Don't be inhuman, have charity
because God on high will reward you.

INSIDE:

You can go now and not bother
because if you anger me I will beat you.

OUTSIDE:

We come very tired from Nazareth
I am the carpenter named Joseph.

INSIDE:

I don't care what your name is, let me sleep
I have told you that we will not open.

OUTSIDE:

We ask for shelter beloved sir
Just one night for the Queen of Heaven.

INSIDE:

Well if a queen is asking
Why is she so alone?

AFUERA:

Mi esposa es María, es Reina del Cielo
Y madre va a ser del Divino Verbo.

ADENTRO:

¿Eres tú, José, tu esposa es María?
Entren peregrinos, no los conocía.

AFUERA:

Dios pague, señores, vuestra caridad
y os colme el cielo de felicidad.

ADENTRO:

Dichosa la casa que alberga este día
a la Virgen pura, la hermosa María.

TODOS:

Entren santos peregrinos, peregrinos,
reciban este rincón,
que aunque pobre la morada, la morada,
os la doy de corazón.

Cantemos con alegría, alegría,
todos al considerar,
que Jesús, José y María,
nos vinieron hoy a honrar.

OUTSIDE:

My wife is Mary, Queen of Heaven
And she is to be mother of the Divine Word.

INSIDE:

Is it you, Joseph, is your wife Mary?
Come in, pilgrims, I didn't recognize you.

OUTSIDE:

God will repay your charity
And fill your skies with happiness.

INSIDE:

Fortunate is the house that shelters this day
The pure Virgin, the beautiful Mary.

EVERYONE:

Come in, holy pilgrims, pilgrims,
you are well received in this corner,
even though the dwelling is humble,
we offer you our hearts.

Let us sing with happiness, happiness,
everyone to consider,
that Jesus, Joseph, and Mary,
today have come to honor us.

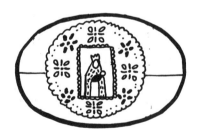

Las Posadas

Performed by El Coro de San José

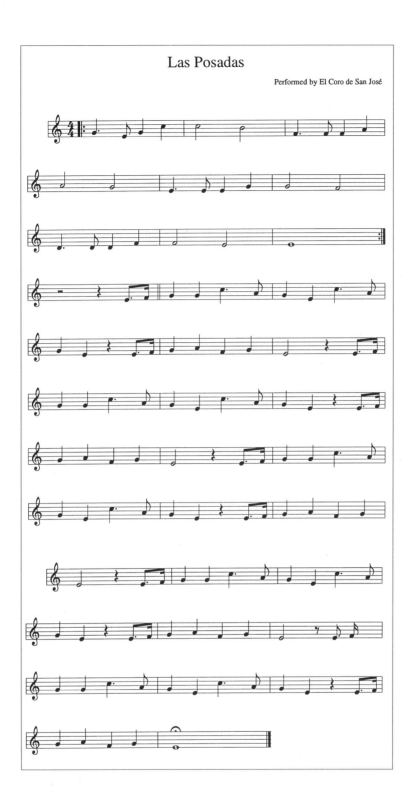

In Latin, *albente caelo* means "at dawn," or literally, "whitening sky." In the Spanish language, *alba* means "dawn." In Nuevo Mexicano Spanish of the Río Grande del Norte, the word *alba* also refers to what Rubén Cobos defines as "a kind of morning song of praise to the dawn." It is sung at the break of dawn after *velorios,* which may be either all-night prayer services for the saints or wakes for the dead. Many people sing the *alba* to begin their day's work. In their voyage into the unknown Atlantic, the crew of Cristóbal Colón sang the *alba* every morning. The dawn was the only thing they were certain of on the first voyage to the Americas.

New Mexico folklorist Enrique R. Lamadrid discovered that his elderly friend, the late Señora Pacífica García, knew a beautiful *alba* that she consented to sing specifically for this publication. Her family has lived in the village of Nambé, New Mexico, for generations, and it is within this bucolic setting that Señora García celebrated every dawning.

Canto al alba	Song to the Dawn
Pacífica García	Pacífica García
Cantemos al alba, ya viene el día. Daremos gracias, Ave María.	Let us sing to the dawn, the day is coming. Let us give thanks, Hail Mary.
Cantemos al alba, ya viene el día. Daremos gracias, Ave María.	Let us sing to the dawn, the day is coming. Let us give thanks, Hail Mary.
Quien al alba canta muy de mañana, indulgencias al cielo gana.	Whoever sings to the dawn early in the morning, will win indulgences from heaven.
En la calle arriba está la custodia. Los ángeles cantan arriba en la gloria.	On the path above is the monstrance. The angels sing above in heaven.
Cantemos al alba, ya viene el día. Daremos gracias, Ave María.	Let us sing to the dawn, the day is coming. Let us give thanks, Hail Mary.
Bendita sea la luz del día. Benditos sean San José y María.	Blessed be the light of day. Blessed be Saint Joseph and Mary.

A la madrugada
nació el Niño Dios.
Al amanecer,
dió su luz el sol.

La mula se espanta
con el resplandor.
El buey con el vaho
calentó al Señor.

Los tres Reyes Magos
del cielo han venido,
a darle las gracias
al Recién Nacido.

El Rey Baltazar
que el era mayor,
presentó el incienso
al Niñito Dios.

Bendita sea
la luz del día.
Bendito sea
Quien nos la envía.

Bendita sea
la claridad.
Bendito sea
Quien nos la da.

Ángel de mi guarda,
noble compañía,
vélame de noche,
guíame en el día.

Cantemos al alba,
ya viene el día.
Daremos gracias,
Ave María.

Estas sí son flores,
estas sí que son.
Gracias a María,
gloria al Señor.

Los gallos cantaron,
las aves salieron.
Toditos los campos
ya se florecieron.

In the early morning
the Infant Lord was born.
At daybreak,
the sun gave its light.

The mule is surprised
at the brilliance.
The ox with his breath
kept the Child warm.

The Three Kings
from heaven have come,
to give thanks
to the One just born.

King Baltazar
was the oldest,
and gave incense
to the God Child.

Blessed be
the light of day.
Blessed be
He that sends it to us.

Blessed be
the clarity.
Blessed be
He that gives it to us.

My guardian angel,
noble company,
watch over me at night,
guide me during the day.

Let us sing to the dawn,
the day is coming.
Let us give thanks,
Hail Mary.

These are truly flowers,
these truly are.
Thanks be to Mary,
glory to the Father.

The roosters crowed,
the birds came out.
All of the fields
are blooming.

Cantemos al alba,	Let us sing to the dawn,
ya viene el día.	day is coming.
Daremos gracias,	Let us give thanks,
Ave María.	Hail Mary.
María divina	Divine Mary
ya no pudo ver	could no longer see
la cuya fiera	the beast
de Lucifer.	Lucifer.
Cantemos al alba,	Let us sing to the dawn,
ya viene el día.	the day is coming.
Daremos gracias,	Let us give thanks,
Ave María.	Hail Mary.

Canto al alba

Performed by Pacífica García

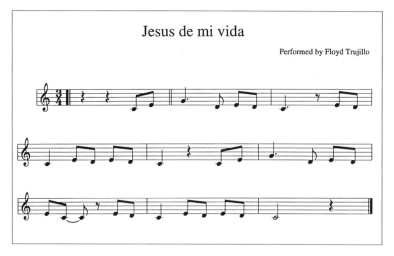

Jesus de mi vida

Performed by Floyd Trujillo

Captain Pérez de Villagrá, the chronicler poet for the expedition of colonization of New Mexico led by Juan de Oñate, wrote that on Holy Thursday in the spring of 1598, the soldiers did penance with scourges while the Franciscan friars, barefoot and garbed in girdles of thorns, chanted hymns and prayed. Unknown to anyone but Villagrá, Oñate found a secluded spot and scourged himself, " … mingling bitter tears with the blood that flowed from his many wounds." Shortly thereafter the Oñate expedition crossed the Río Grande into what would become New Mexico.

The brothers of the *Hermandad de Nuestro Padre Jesús Nazareno,* popularly known as the "*penitentes,*" are greatly misunderstood by those who live outside their religious province. Some scholars believe this sect had its genesis in Europe in the thirteenth century. Others have noticed that documentary evidence of the Brotherhood appears suddenly in the late eighteenth century in New Mexico. Because of the secrecy and privacy that surrounds it, this ancient Christian tradition prevails with an air of deep mystery throughout the region. I once asked a friend who is an *hermano* where in northern New Mexico might there be *moradas,* or chapels, where the *hermanos* perform many of their devotions. He chuckled and with a twinkle in his eye said, "Probably everywhere there's a zip code."

Until recent times, the "*penitente*" tradition has been enshrouded in secrecy for political as well as spiritual reasons. Their practices did not meet with the approval of the Catholic clerical hierarchy in the nineteenth century. Conceivably the church hierarchy felt that it was losing control, because the *hermanos* had assumed much of the responsibility for maintaining the Christian tradition in a region infrequently visited by clerics. Whatever the reasons, the internecine conflict seems to have healed, for I have met Catholic priests who are also members of the Brotherhood.

Of the publications that have appeared on the subject, one of the most comprehensive and objective is *Brothers of Light, Brothers of Blood,* by Marta Weigle. I know this book to be highly regarded, because a friend of mine who is an *hermano mayor,* or elder brother, frequently refers to it as a historical source.

It was the *hermanos* who helped sustain the Christian tradition in the Hispano villages through the long centuries of isolation from trained clerics. They still perform functions vital to the well-being of their respective communities throughout the year, although they are best known for the devotions they observe each *Semana Santa,* or Holy Week. They provide aid to those in need by ministering to the ailing, presenting sustenance to the needy, and assuming responsibility for the good of the community by conducting funerals or otherwise working where they feel their presence is necessary. They perform within a context of mutual cooperation that turn-of-the-century anarchist philosopher Peter Kropotkin would have deemed ideal for the maintenance of the community.

There is a musical form known as the *alabado,* or hymn of praise, that is sung by the *hermanos* as they perform their services. According to Richard Stark, there are few direct connections between the *alabados* of Spain and New Mexico; indeed, no one knows for certain the origins of these New Mexican hymns. They are sung to a very slow, mournful tempo and sometimes seem modal in their melody lines, reflecting what some regard as a Moorish or possibly Sephardic influence. It should be recalled that the Sephardic Jews were expelled from Spain in 1492, and many came to the New World in the guise of Christians, hoping to avoid the horrors of the Spanish Inquisition. The melody is simple and repetitive, going on for many stanzas. There is no instrumental accompaniment; however, a *pito,* which is symbolic of the wail of the Virgin María and the blessed souls of Purgatory, is sometimes played between the stanzas of an individual *alabado.* The *pito* is a fipple instrument resembling the soprano recorder and is handcrafted of wood by the individual *pitero.* Because the construction of these instruments follows no formula, any two may not tune to each other.

The singers of the *alabados* possess notebooks containing their musical repertoires. Some of the *hermanos* have expressed concern that old melodies may be forgotten. *Alabados*, some of which are extremely long, are sung in context with the performance of the ritual.

At the time of recording, Floyd Trujillo was the *hermano mayor* of the *morada* in Abiquiú, New Mexico. Señor Trujillo sings these hymns with great beauty, adopting the attitudes necessary for achieving a level of spiritual consciousness that is correct for this deepest religious expression. Presented here is Floyd Trujillo's rendering of the *penitente alabado Jesús de mi vida*. When it is sung in a group setting, an antiphonal style is used, in which each successive stanza is sung by a lead singer, who is then answered by the rest of the group, repeating the first stanza as a chorus.

Jesús de mi vida

Floyd Trujillo

Jesús de mi vida,
de mi corazón,
ya vas de partida,
Divino Señor.

Jesús, Nuestro Padre,
Vuestro Señor,
ya vas de partida,
Divino Señor.

Con grillos de esposas
le atan pies y manos,
lloran sus tormentos
todos los cristianos.

Con suma paciencia,
Divino Señor,
está Vuestra Madre
con tanto dolor.

Ya lo sentenciaron,
llegan los lacayos,
llegan los judíos
que no son cristianos.

Aquí vino Judas,
ya llegó rabiando,
y a él echan las manos,
ya lo van sacando.

Jesus of My Life

Floyd Trujillo

Jesus of my life,
of my heart,
you are already departing,
Divine Lord.

Jesus, Our Father,
Your Lord,
you are already departing,
Divine Lord.

With shackles and cuffs
they tie his feet and hands,
his torments are mourned
by all Christians.

With total patience,
Divine Lord,
there is Your Mother,
with so much pain.

They already sentenced Him,
the foot soldiers arrive,
the Jews arrive
who are not Christians.

Here came Judas,
he came raving,
and they lay hands on him,
already they take him away.

Por la calle amarga
ya lo van paseando,
con golpes y risas
ya lo están moqueando.

Con qué sentimiento
Divino Señor,
está Vuestra Madre
con tan cruel dolor.

¡Ay, Madre amorosa
de mi corazón,
Madre Dolorosa
llena de aflicción!

¿Vistes a Vuestro Hijo
ya tan fatigado,
con la cruz a cuestas
tres veces ha caído?

¿Vistes el lienzo
con que le limpiaron
aquellos verdugos
cuando lo amarraron?

Ya temió la muerte
el dulce Jesús
cuando lo bajaron
de la Santa Cruz.

Están sus discípulos,
ellos lo entregaron,
y los fariseos
lo crucificaron.

Suenan sus trompetas
¡qué gusto han tenido
de ver a Jesús
que venía herido!

Le dan puñaladas
con soberbia e ira
y con tanta injuria
le quitan la vida.

Mi Dios humillado,
único Señor,
fueron las lanzadas
en su corazón.

Down the bitter street
they are parading Him,
with blows and laughter
they are already lashing Him.

With what sentiment,
Divine Lord,
is Your Mother there
with such cruel pain.

Oh, loving Mother
of my heart,
Sorrowful Mother
full of affliction.

Did you see Your Son
already so tired,
with the cross on His shoulder
three times He has fallen?

Did you see the cloth
with which they wiped Him,
those executioners
when they tied Him?

He already feared death
sweet Jesus
when they took Him down
from the Holy Cross.

There are his disciples,
they surrendered Him,
and the Pharisees
crucified Him.

The trumpets sound,
what pleasure they have had
seeing Jesus
who came wounded!

They stab Him
with arrogance and rage
and with much injury
take away His life.

My humiliated God,
only Lord,
the lance thrusts
went to Your heart.

San Juan y la Virgen ya se han desmayado de ver a Jesús, cómo lo han mortificado.	Saint John and the Virgin have already fainted from seeing Jesus, how they have tortured Him.
La preciosa sangre de mi Redentor, sufrió con tormento su muerte y pasión.	The precious blood of my Redeemer, suffered with torment His death and passion.
O, dichosa Madre que con mucho anhelo vistes a Vuestro Hijo el Rey de los Cielos.	Oh, fortunate Mother who with much desire saw Your Son the King of Heaven.
Este Niño hermoso este, mi Lucero, el Rey de los Cielos y del mundo entero.	This beautiful Child this, my Star, the King of Heaven and of the whole world.
Por su gran poder nos vino la luz, fue cuando José lo apeó de la cruz.	By His great power light came to us, it was when Joseph lowered Him from the cross.
Con temor, victoria que tenemos luz alaben el nombre del dulce Jesús.	With fear, victory we have light praise the name of sweet Jesus.
Vamos ofreciendo en la Santa Cruz, vamos adorando al dulce Jesús.	Let us make offering at the Holy Cross, let us adore sweet Jesus.
Amén.	*Amen.*

Burial is the final ritual of death, and the *despedimientos,* or traditional grave-side farewell hymns, are profoundly moving. They are preserved and performed by the *penitente* brothers, who not only take charge of important rituals like funerals, but also look after the welfare of bereaved or needy families. In *Adiós, acompañamiento,* "Farewell, Companions," the singer takes on the voice of the deceased taking leave of friends and family, one by one.

Adiós, acompañamiento

Russell Madrid

¡Adiós, acompañamiento,
donde me estaban velando,
ya se llegó la hora y tiempo
de que me vayan sacando!

¡Adiós, mis amados padres
que conservaban mi vida,
ya se llegó la hora y tiempo,
ya se llegó mi partida!

¡Qué corazones no sienten,
tan solo en considerar,
que este paso tan amargo
todos lo tienen que andar!

La sepultura es mi cama,
la tierra mi propio ser,
se me atemoriza el alma
de considerarme en él.

¡Adiós, todos mis parientes,
toditos en general
encomienden mi alma a Dios,
no me vayan a olvidar!

Farewell, Companions

Russell Madrid

Farewell, companions,
where they watched over me
the hour and time have come
to take me out!

Farewell, my beloved parents
who conserved my life,
the hour and time have come,
my parting is here!

What hearts do not feel,
just in considering,
that this bitter step
will be taken by all!

My tomb is my bed,
the earth is my being,
my soul trembles
to see me in it.

Farewell, all my relatives,
everyone in general
commend my soul to God,
do not forget me!

Adiós, acompañamiento

Sung by Russell Madrid

One of the most meaningful events in a human lifetime is the sacrament of marriage. This is the foundation of the family and results in the perpetuation of the bloodlines and the cultural traditions of the wedded couple. The solemnity with which the wedding ceremony is performed in Hispano Catholic churches probes deeply into the mystery of the *coniunctio oppositorum*, the conjoining of opposites, the marriage of the male and the female. The documentary film *Celebración del matrimonio*, "Celebration of Marriage," produced by Margaret Hixon (1986), portrays the wedding and the symbolism within this sacred tradition.

Immediately after the wedding is the *fiesta de los novios*, which is a secular reception involving the entire community. This fiesta is as profound in its own way as the actual wedding ceremony presided over by the priest. Within the old tradition, a procession of the wedding party and congregation wends from the church to the place of the reception. The *músicos*, traditionally a *violinista* and a *guitarrista*, play the *Marcha de los novios*, the processional march of the newlyweds.

On arriving at the reception hall, the *músicos*, still playing the march, go to their appointed places while the *procesión* continues, led by a married couple who are close friends or relatives of the newlyweds. The *procesión* continues, comprised of the bride, the groom, *padres, padrinos, abuelos, tíos y tías, hermanos y hermanas, primos y primas, amigos y amigas*—all following the lead couple as they wind, serpentlike, now in two lines, now both lines joining hands in a long, human canopy, now spiraling this way and that, all to the beat of the *Marcha de los novios*. Finally the *marcha* finishes, and the serpent dissociates into its myriad human parts who seek their own places, the men searching out each other's company, often quaffing *cerveza* to settle the dust in the gullets and recharge for the next phase of the festivities. The women, as if by magic, unveil the food, carefully prepared beforehand, food that reflects a culinary art form collectively arranged, a collage of *chile, posole, tamales, frijoles, enchiladas, carne adovada, burritos, ensaladas, tortillas, sopaipillas, salsas, biscochitos, empanaditas*—an overwhelming array of wondrous food that has sustained this culture for centuries—food that tastes this way only in the north country, where the recipes have evolved in harmony with the yield of *la tierra*, the earth.

After everyone has eaten from this feast of plenty, it is time for the singing of *La entriega de los novios*. The *entregador/a* is a man or woman who lives in the area and is noted for a special rendition of this traditional, secular rite of passage into the state of matrimony. The *entriega* is very long, often lasting an hour or more, as the *entregador/a* sings the *versos* that define the conduct and states of mind necessary for the success of marriage. Among *la gente* of the region is the tradition of being wedded again on the fiftieth anniversary. After the second wedding, the reception is held as it was fifty years before.

Toward the end of *La entriega de los novios*, individual *versos* are sung that mention specific members of the community by name. These *versos* often elicit applause and laughter. If an individual is left out, negative feelings may result, so the *entregador/a* is careful to apologize for any mistakes or omissions. At the end of the performance of *La entriega de los novios*, the *entregador/a*, looking somewhat exhausted from the extraordinary effort of sustained singing, graciously thanks the audience and withdraws. The *músicos* strike up the wedding waltz, and the newly wedded couple dance alone for awhile, rapt in this unforgettable moment of genesis. And then a man cuts in, to dance briefly with the bride and wish her well by pinning a dollar to her wedding gown. He is followed by another and yet another and another, until her wedding gown is a paper salad of bills that will help launch the couple on their honeymoon. By now the dance floor is filled with dancing couples, and the *baile* has begun that will last far into the night, a night filled with myriad adventures, amorous and otherwise.

The *Marcha de los novios* included here was performed by Abenicio Montoya on the violin and Benny Bustos on the guitar. This is an old *marcha,* traditionally performed around Santa Fe. Señor Bustos described their traditional performance of this march from the church to the place of the wedding reception only days before this recording was made. Señor Montoya was known by many of the elderly *gente* of Santa Fe as one of the most popular *músicos* of the last sixty years.

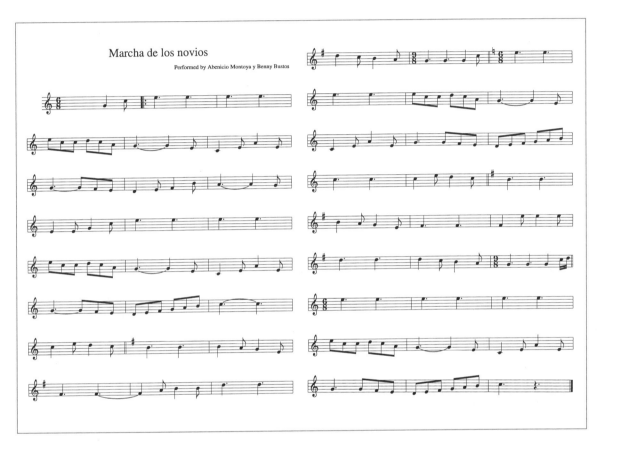

Marcha de los novios

Performed by Abenicio Montoya y Benny Bustos

The (abbreviated) version of *La entriega de los novios* presented here was performed by Cipriano Vigil, who is undoubtedly one of New Mexico's greatest performing folk musicians. Señor Vigil has made a lifelong study of this form.

La entriega de los novios

Cipriano Vigil

"Ave María," dijo el ave
para empezar a volar,
"Ave María," digo yo
para empezar a cantar.

A Dios le pido licencia,
memoria y sabiduría,
para formar el estado
que se ha formado este día.

Esta mañana salieron
cuatro flores a la iglesia,
el padrino y la madrina,
el novio y su princesa.

¿Qué significan las arras
cuando las van a usar?
Significa el mismo cuerpo
que allí se van a juntar.

Cristo nos dio a conocer
que él padeció en su morada,
llevó la cruz con esmero
como a su esposa adorada.

El matrimonio es legal
con la voluntad de dos,
el matrimonio es bonito
con la voluntad de Dios.

El matrimonio es delicado
como un vaso de cristal,
no más una vez se rompe
ya no se puede juntar.

Óigame usted, el esposado,
lo que le voy a decir:
"Tiene a su princesa a su lado,
Dios la sabe bendecir."

The Delivery of the Newlyweds

Cipriano Vigil

The bird says, "Ave María,"
to begin its flight.
I say, "Ave María,"
to begin to sing.

From God I ask license,
memory, and wisdom,
to form the state
which has been formed today.

This morning emerged
four flowers from the church,
the godparents,
the groom and his princess.

What do the coins signify
when they are used?
They symbolize the same body
that there will be joined.

Christ made it known to us
that He suffered in his dwelling place,
He carried the cross with great care
like a beloved wife.

Marriage is legal
with the consent of both partners,
marriage is beautiful
with the will of God.

Marriage is delicate
like a crystal glass,
if it is broken even once,
it cannot be mended.

Listen to me, new husband,
to what I have to tell you:
"You have your princess at your side,
God knows how to bless her."

Óigame usted, la esposada,
lo que le voy a cantar:
"Tiene a su novio a su lado,
no lo vaya a abandonar."

Este versito que canto
se lo dedico al padrino,
el estado en que se encuentra
es un estado divino.

Por este río para abajo
corre el agua cristalina
donde se lavan las manos
el padrino y la madrina.

Del cielo bajó un pintor
para pintar tu hermosura
Señora Eufrasia Romero,
de esto está usted segura.

Y con este me despido,
dispensen lo mal trovado.
Aquí tienen sus hijitos
están ellos entregados.

Listen to me, new wife,
to what I have to sing you:
"You have your husband at your side,
do not abandon him."

This little verse that I sing
I dedicate to the godfather,
the state that you are in
is a divine state.

Downstream in this river
flows the crystalline water
where the godparents
wash their hands.

An artist descended from heaven
to paint your beauty,
Señora Eufrasia Romero,
of this you can be certain.

And with this I bid you farewell,
please pardon the singing.
Here you have your children
they are now delivered.

La entriega de los novios

Performed by Cipriano Vigil

CHAPTER SIX

La Música de los Bailes

MUCH OF THE MUSICAL REPERTOIRE of *la gente* in the region of the Río Grande del Norte is the music performed for *bailes,* or dances. These memorable gatherings provided regular highlights of community life and were one of the few entertainments available to villagers. Almost everyone in a village who could attend would be there, old and young. Courtships were conducted under the watchful but sympathetic eyes of elders and everyone else. The master of ceremonies, or *bastonero* (literally the man with the cane), maintained and directed the energies of the occasion and often collected donations for the musicians. As Rubén Cobos has described, he also presided over a popular game called *el valse chiquiado,* "the coaxing waltz." After stopping the music, the *bastonero* would select a couple, who were then obliged to recite or improvise verses that usually revealed to all how the pair felt about each other. One partner sat in a chair while the other attempted to coax him or her to resume dancing. Some verses are touching and sentimental while others are hilarious. Moments were created that people remembered the rest of their lives. A group of senior citizens in El Rancho, New Mexico, recited the following verses for Enrique R. Lamadrid. In this interchange first the man expresses his devotion then the woman complains about his past behavior:

ÉL:

Tengo una sala medida
con cien yardas de listón,
en cada esquina una rosa
y en medio tu corazón.

HE:

I have a hall measured out
with a hundred yards of ribbon,
in each corner a rose
and in the middle your heart.

ELLA:

Dices que me quieres tanto
pero esto no es verdad,
porque el modo que tú te portas
es una barbaridad.

SHE:

You say you love me so
but this is not true,
because the way you behave
is a disgrace.

Unfazed and determined, he tries to lure her into dancing by lighting a candle to her love. She denies him again with a beautiful and well known couplet designed to entice him even more:

EL:

En la orilla de una laguna
prendí una vela al momento,
si quiere bailar conmigo
levántese de ese asiento.

ELLA:

De las estrellas del cielo
voy a bajarle dos,
una para saludarte
y otra para decirte adiós.

HE:

On the shores of a lake
I lit a candle in a moment,
if you want to dance with me
get up out of that chair.

SHE:

Of the stars in the sky
I will bring down two for you,
one to greet you
and the other to say farewell.

The dance music that has been enjoyed for generations in New Mexico has a long history. Traditionally this music has been performed on violin and guitar, neither of which had assumed its current form when Fray Pedro de Gante established his schools of music in Mexico in the 1520s. It was not until the beginning of the baroque era (1600–1750) that the modern violin came into currency with its tuning of g, d', a' and e".

In his *"Syntagma musicum"* (1618), Michael Praetorius distinguishes this as the modern violin. Violins from the sixteenth century are regarded as rare to nonexistent by most authorities.

The guitar has existed in one form or another for at least eight centuries. The "Gate of Glory" to the Church of Santiago de Compostela in Spain, rendered by Master Mateo, displays a guitar-shaped instrument thought to be a *vihuela*, the old Spanish viol, or guitar. However, it was not until about 1790 that the Spanish guitar assumed its current tuning E, A, d, g, b, e".

The written notation is placed an octave higher, that is e, a, d', g', b', e".

At the time of the conquest, three distinct types of *vihuela* were played. The *vihuela de péndola* was played with a plectrum, as is the modern mandolin. The *vihuela de arco* was played with a bow, as is the viol. The *vihuela de mano,* which was played with the hand, became ubiquitous in Spain at the time of the conquest, and a great deal of music was arranged for it. In all probability the latter two instruments were included in the schools of Pedro de Gante.

The music that Aurora Lucero-White regarded as appropriate for the Spanish-colonial dances did not actually find its way into the region of the Río Grande del Norte until the midnineteenth century during the brief and disastrous reign of Maximilian. Much of this music came to the New World from the salons of Paris, where cues of fashion were generated by the Empress Eugenie, wife of Napoleon III. It worked its way northward from Mexico, where it melded with the tradition of *la gente,* who claim it as their own and who play it to this day. This music came to be performed in the *salas,* or drawing rooms, of the well-to-do of northern New Mexico and southern Colorado. According to Lucero-White, it was in these *salas* that "the elite met; there, under crystal candelabra, their images reflected in long mirrors, they danced; their war, love, politics were discussed; their trades were consummated; fortunes were made and lost. But always decorum was maintained; always rhythm modulated the life patterns of the company even as rhythm modulated their dance steps."

The *bailes* were held frequently, whether in the *salas* of Santa Fe, with its sense of the cosmopolitan, or in the villages scattered throughout the mountains and along the rivers. The *tonadillas,* or tunes, were passed from *músico* to *músico* through memory rather than written musical notation. No wonder that the melodies wandered through seemingly endless permutations as the character of each passing musician embellished a given song. New melodies were composed within the forms that had come to prevail. Polkas, waltzes, schottisches, quadrilles, and varsovianas became New Mexican even though their place of genesis was the span of an ocean away.

With the coming of the railroad in the last decades of the nineteenth century came violins manufactured in Germany bearing a label reading:

ANTONIUS
STRADIVARIUS
CREMONENTIS
FACIEBAT ANNO 1716
MADE IN GERMANY

These violins are now found throughout New Mexico and southern Colorado, and some of the *violinistas* regard them to have been fashioned by the master himself, thus perpetuating a myth of the violin's great worth. After a century of use, these instruments have become incorporated into the tradition of Hispano music. In the dance music included in this work, one may hear many approaches to performing on the violin and guitar. The entire array gives a fair portrayal of *la música de los bailes* within this strangely isolated tradition. There is no music that conveys the sense of this musical tradition more accurately nor more poignantly than the violin/guitar performances of *la música de los viejitos*.

The transcriptions are generally of the melodies as performed by the *violinistas*. Repeats are indicated, but variations have not been transcribed because the music can be heard on the CD albums. Certain aspects of technique are noted; for example the violin performances of the late Vicente Montoya were particularly noted for their use of double stops. The late Ventura Rael performed with a definite crispness and anticipation of the beat without loss of rhythmic integrity. As Reed Cooper has aptly noted, some measures may gain or lose beats within the time signature. I have indicated instances of this by marking such measures with broken measure lines. Cooper raised the obvious question: what happens to the dancers when the *músicos* arbitrarily change the number of beats per measure? I have watched dancers accommodate this phenomenon with great decorum. They simply dance to the beat of their own tradition.

I have transcribed the music in the key in which the *músicos* performed. They were not necessarily tuned to A 440. In some instances the music may be as much as three half tones off pitch. In the performance of folk music, tuning is relative.

Of the folk dances included in the present work, none has enjoyed a greater popularity in the Río Grande del Norte than *La varsoviana*, "the girl from Warsaw." To date we have recorded no less than thirty-six versions of the melody, which was regarded by the late, gifted folk musician Vicente Montoya as *la música de los viejitos*. We subsequently applied this title to our series of over one hundred radio programs based on our field recordings. *La varsoviana* was the theme song for that series.

Ironically this dance did not originate in New Mexico, as so many New Mexicans believe. It is thought to be of French origin, having evolved from the *mazurka*, itself a form of Polish folk song and country dance that carries from the plains of Mazowsze, the area in which Warsaw is located. *La varsoviana* is thought to have been introduced in Paris by the dance master Désiré in 1853 and is purported to have become a favorite of the Empress Eugenie, wife of Napoleon III. Napoleon's agent, Archduke Maximilian, briefly presided as emperor of Mexico from 1863 to 1867, when Mexico came under French domination. His wife, Carlotta, was quick to take any cue from Eugenie as to what was fashionable in the salons of Paris. Thus much of the repertoire of dance music still performed by *la gente* del Río Grande del Norte is directly attributable to Carlotta and Eugenie. It is not unreasonable to suppose that *La varsoviana*, or *La Varsouvienne*, as it was then known, made its way first to the New World and then northward into the hearts of *la gente*. This is a perfect example of what the eminent Argentine ethnomusicologist Carlos Vega refers to as the process of "folklorization"—the progress of music and dance from the salons of eighteenth and nineteenth century Europe to the far reaches and harsh environments of the New World.

La varsoviana is in 3/4 time and AABB form. The melody is thirty-two measures long and is repeated several times. At the beginning of the dance, the couples are positioned in a line, one couple behind the other, all facing forward. Each man is to the left of his partner. He holds her left hand in his own, while his right arm is extended above and behind her shoulders, to hold her right hand. As the pickup notes signal the beginning of the melody, everyone's left foot is raised and comes down on the first beat of the first measure, stepping with the right foot on the second beat, hopping on the right foot on the third beat. This process is repeated in the second measure; then the couples step left-right-left to the three beats of the third measure. On the first beat of the fourth measure, the right foot comes to rest, pointing slightly outward. On the third beat of this measure, the woman shifts to the man's left, so that by the fifth measure they are reversed from the position in which they began. Through the next four measures, they repeat the steps of the first four but leading with the opposite foot, so that by the beginning of the ninth measure they have assumed their original relative positions. From the ninth through sixteenth measures, they repeat the steps of the first eight measures, thereby completing the AA portions of the melody. In the second half of the melody, beginning from their original position, the couples step to the beat of the melody as follows: left-right-left, right-rest-rest, right-left-right, left-rest-rest, etc.

Throughout the BB portions of the melody, the man and woman shift positions from left to right and back again every odd measure, so that they have assumed their original positions by the end of the sixteenth measure. The number of repetitions of the dance from this point is left to the discretion of the *músicos.*

The version of *La varsoviana* included here was performed on the violin by the late Vicente Montoya and on the guitar by Margarito Olivas, both of whom were well known around Las Vegas, New Mexico, for many years.

Dance positions are keyed to music on following page.

↗ = direction of movement while shifting from one side to the other

= Female dancer

= Male dancer

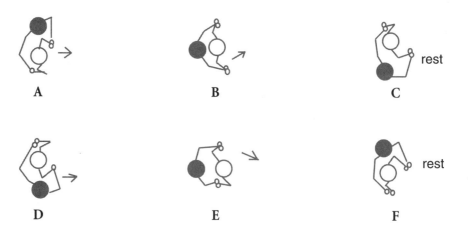

A B C

D E F

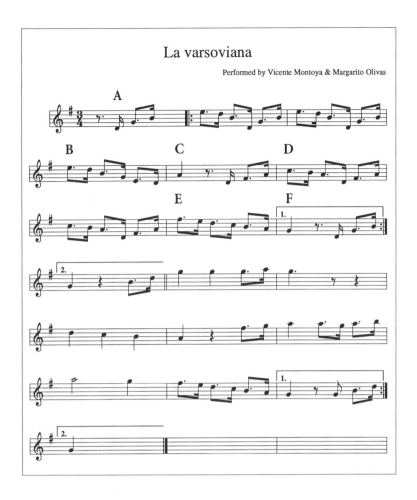

La varsoviana

Performed by Vicente Montoya & Margarito Olivas

As with many of the other dances that still prevail among *la gente,* the origins of the *valse,* or waltz, are difficult to determine. Etymologically the German word *waltzen* is related to the Latin *volvere,* which in its broadest sense means to "cause to revolve, roll, turn about, turn around." Both *waltzen* and *volvere* seem to be descended from a common Indo-European ancestor. It is thought that the origins of the *valse* may be traced to the Alpine spring dances of the Bavarian Highlands and Upper Austria. These early peasant dances were fraught with wild hopping and throwing of the female partner up into the air or over the shoulder. The melodies were either sung or performed on Alpine instruments such as the alphorn, the shepherd's pipe, or the shawm. The tunes were originally work songs to accompany the rhythm of sowing or reaping that claimed much of the attention of the peasant folk. Many of these dances were gloriously erotic, as these people who lived within the flow of Nature responded to the unleashing of their vernal urges. This natural eroticism pervading many peasant dances came to be considered the "invention of the devil" by religious and civil authorities, who sought a more chaste veneer for civilization as a means of ordering the apparent chaos of Nature.

As these dances gradually became part of the repertoire of a given community, they lost some of their rustic ardor. The dances became more sophisticated, but many of the cultured townfolk began to assume what were regarded to be more simple and natural characteristics as they performed these dances.

The *valse*, or waltz, first appeared between 1770 and 1780 and was danced by everyone from the rich to the poor—noblemen to commoners. It arose at a time when the spirit of human rights was emerging in the ferment that resulted in the French Revolution. A traveler from Bavaria had this to say:

> The people here are excessively fond of the pleasure of dancing; they need only to hear the music of the waltz to begin to caper, no matter where they are. The public dance floors are visited by all classes; … Here we see artisans, artists, merchants, councilors, barons, counts and excellencies dancing together with waitresses, women of the middle class and ladies. Every stranger who stays here for awhile is infected with this dance malady.

Inasmuch as the *valses* swept Europe in the late eighteenth century, it is conceivable that they arrived in the New World shortly thereafter, preceding the brief reign of Maximilian. They made an enormous musical impact and were elevated to a monumental status by composers and performers of the Viennese waltz. By the late nineteenth century, Mexican composers were writing *valses* in the Viennese style.

A waltz that has long been included in the Hispano tradition of the Río Grande del Norte was composed by a young Mexican in the latter years of the nineteenth century. *Sobre las olas*, known in English as "Over the Waves," was written by Juventino Rosas, a gifted *violinista* who died in 1894 at the age of twenty-six. Rosas wrote this waltz in 1891 after the fashion of the Viennese waltz. It was tremendously popular in both Mexico and Europe. "Over the Waves" became well known throughout the United States and was a hit in the 1940s, when lyrics were added and it became known as "The Loveliest Night of the Year."

This version of *Sobre las olas* was performed by Abenicio Montoya and Benny Bustos of Santa Fe. *Sobre las olas* was traditionally performed as the wedding waltz around Santa Fe.

In New Mexico and southern Colorado, the *valses* and *redondos,* or round dances, are still performed wherever the elderly *gente* gather to attend social dances. The *redondos* are performed to melodies in a stately 3/4 time with distinct A and B sections. In the A section the couples form a circle holding hands, and the circle revolves as the dancers' feet move to the waltz step. In the B section the circle breaks into couples who dance the waltz in the ballroom position. As the A section of the melody resumes, the couples regroup in the revolving circle without breaking the waltz step, and so on until the musicians conclude playing.

A *redondo* performed around Taos is called *El valse de don Gorgonio.* The late José Damián Archuleta recounted the story that Eliza, his wife, had an uncle named Antonio C. Pacheco, who was at one time a New Mexico state senator from Taos County. Senator Pacheco was noted for his good humor and sociability. One night many years ago in the village of Arroyo Seco, *la gente* were having a *baile,* and the *músicos* were Miguel Salazar on the violin and Andrés Sánchez on the guitar. Both men were blind. All of the villagers were assembled, including the *viejo* Don Gorgonio, who made daily trips into the mountains to gather firewood, which he loaded onto the back of his *burro.* For some time Senator Pacheco had liked to call attention to his old friend Don Gorgonio, and when the *músicos* struck up the melody for a *redondo,* the good senator proclaimed that hereafter the melody would be known as *El valse de don Gorgonio.* Now decades later, the *músicos,* Senator Pacheco, and Don Gorgonio have passed from this world, but Don Gorgonio has been immortalized in the *valse* that honors his name.

The version of *El valse de don Gorgonio* presented here was performed by José Damián Archuleta on the violin and Pablo Trujillo on the guitar. Their version of this melody appears in the documentary films *Los Alegres* and *La Música de los Viejos.*

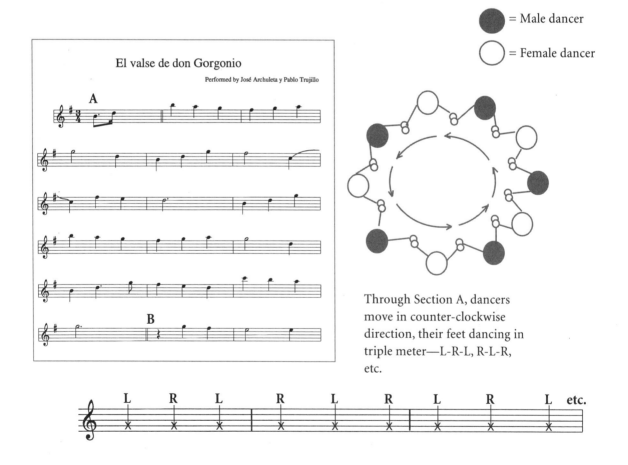

● = Male dancer

○ = Female dancer

El valse de don Gorgonio

Performed by José Archuleta y Pablo Trujillo

A

B

Through Section A, dancers move in counter-clockwise direction, their feet dancing in triple meter—L-R-L, R-L-R, etc.

L R L R L R L R L etc.

El valse de don Gorgonio

(continued)

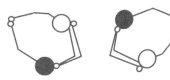

Through section B, dancers break into couples and dance in ballroom position.

One of the most graceful and spectacular of the Hispano folk dances is *El valse de los paños*. The dance requires that the melody has both A and B sections. This *valse* is performed by groups of six dancers. Each group of six is divided into two facing rows of two women and one man. The two trios face each other. Each man holds a bandanna (*paño)* in both his left and right hands, and stands between his two female partners. The lady to his right holds the other end of one *paño* in her left hand, while the lady to his left holds the other end of her *pano* in her right hand. The *tonadilla*, or melody, begins, and the two trios dance with waltz steps forward toward each other for four measures, then backwards away from each other for the second four measures. This sequence is repeated to complete the sixteen measures in the A section.

In the B section, the dancers hold their *paños* high, and the woman to the man's left dances in front of him, preceding him through the arch formed by the elevated *paño* he holds with the woman to his right. The man revolves one full turn clockwise, and then the woman on his right mirrors this procedure by dancing in front of him toward the left, beneath the arch on the man's left, and again the man dances a full revolution, this time counter-clockwise. At this point the trios are all facing forward again, but the *paños* are twisted. In order to untwist them, this entire procedure must be exactly reversed, at which point section B has been completed.

The A and B patterns alternate until the music, in 3/4 time and AB form, stops. In the version performed by José Damián Archuleta and Pablo Trujillo, the A section is sixteen measures long and the B section is eighteen measures long. It is possible that the B section has two additional measures to allow the dancers extra time to complete the intricate moves in this section.

The performance of *El valse de los paños* presented here appears in the documentary film *Los Alegres*.

Valse de los paños

Performed by José Archuleta y Pablo Trujillo

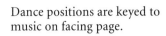

Dance positions are keyed to music on facing page.

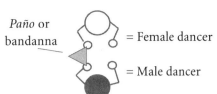

= direction of movement

Paño or bandanna

= Female dancer

= Male dancer

A

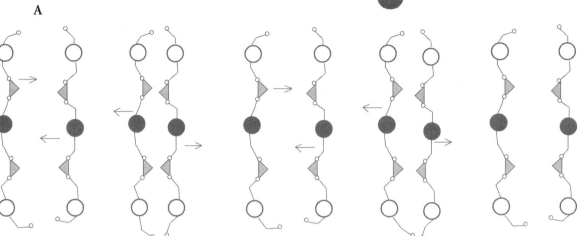

L R L R L R L R L R L R repeat 12 more measures

B

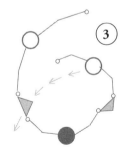

①

②

③

④

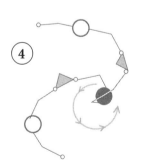

LRL RLR
1

LRL RLR
2

LRL RLR
3

LRL RLR
4

José D. Romero, of Las Vegas, New Mexico, recalls that long ago, as a boy herding sheep and goats, he came upon the abandoned neck of a guitar. He took it home and fashioned a wooden soundbox, which he attached to the neck. He gathered the entrails of slaughtered livestock which he twisted and dried to form gut strings. He mounted these on his new instrument and then taught himself to play the guitar. Señor Romero went on to learn to play the violin and mandolin. His son, Remijio Romero, is one of the best traditional Hispano guitar players in New Mexico. One of the *valses* played by the father-son duet was *El valse Noriega*.

In the version of *El valse Noriega* presented here, the late José Domingo Romero plays the violin, accompanied on the guitar by his son Remijio. Folklorist Adrian Treviño has pointed out that the melody line is reminiscent of *The Carnival of Venice*. The provenance of this *valse* is forgotten, but it may have been performed in its current form by someone named Noriega. In one section of the melody, Señor Romero employs an unusual ricochet technique of bowing in place of the usual legato style.

El valse Noriega

Performed by José D. y Remijio Romero

(Continued on next page)

El valse Noriega
(continued)

Guadalupe Urioste was born in 1907. He spent much of his life in Las Vegas, New Mexico, where he was well known as a *violinista*. He loved to play old Hispano folk music and early country-western music, particularly songs written by Jimmie Rodgers. His repertoire included some very old dance tunes that he said had been in his family for generations. Señor Urioste knew the *valse* included here as *El valse rabino,* or "The Rabbi's Waltz," which raises some interesting speculation as to its provenance. Historians E. A. Mares and Tomás Atencio have mentioned in conversation that collectors of the Hispano folk music of this region should attend to the possibility of Sephardic influence; when the Sephardic Jews were expelled from Spain in 1492, many are thought to have migrated to the New World to avoid the pogroms that prevailed in Europe even into the twentieth century. This waltz has an unusual melody line that is more appropriately accommodated by a 6/8 time signature.

Señor Urioste was the only *violinista* we have recorded who knew this *valse,* and he passed away on June 26, 1981, on his way to perform at a *baile* where we were to record him. The mystery of the origins of this song remains unsolved.* Señor Urioste was accompanied on the guitar by a well-known folk musician from Las Vegas, José Geraldo Martínez.

El valse rabino

Performed by Guadalupe Urioste y José G. Martínez

* However, when I whistled this waltz to a knowledgeable Basque folk musician she recognized the melody as one she had heard many times in Basque country in the Pyrenees mountains. She also stated that Urioste is a Basque name.

The polka is thought to have evolved from central European peasant dances, first as a round dance. "The polka (Polish girl) is undoubtedly of Polish origin," according to the Groves Dictionary; however, it is thought by Dr. Tobias Norlind that the polka "was originated by the Poles domiciled in southern Hungary … In the first years of its existence, the polka was treated as a Hungarian folk dance." The musical characteristics of the polka assumed their current form around 1800 and many polkas were written down to be used by village musicians and schoolmasters. In 1837 the polka social dance involving couples was introduced in Prague and by 1839 had made its way to Vienna and St. Petersburg. In 1840 it was danced in the Théâtre de l'Odéon in Paris and shortly thereafter became the rage of Parisian society. In 1844 it migrated to both London and the United States, and in 1845, when James Knox Polk became the eleventh president of the United States, polka jokes ran rampant.

It was during the period of Polk's presidency that the Mexican–American War resulted in the United States gaining vast lands from Mexico under the terms of the Treaty of Guadalupe Hidalgo dated February 2, 1848. Part of the lands included in both this treaty and the Gadsden Purchase of 1853 were to become the state of New Mexico in 1912.

The polka may well have arrived in New Mexico from both the east and the south at about the same time in the midnineteenth century. It immediately gained great popularity with *la gente*, and to this day it is frequently danced at *los bailes* in the Río Grande del Norte. It is in 2/4 time to a somewhat slow military march tempo, the quarter note equaling 104 by standard metronomic measure. Although the polka had its origins within the repertoire of folk dance, it has also been incorporated into classical composition.

The polka is danced by couples, the couples dancing left-right-left-hop, right-left-right-hop within the measure.

Señor Ventura Rael was born in Mimbres, New Mexico, in 1907. He was one of New Mexico's greatest Hispano fiddlers and displayed a highly developed musical sense. His attention to intonation and rhythmic correctness was rare among folk musicians. His style was to play just ahead of the beat, phrasing with great sensitivity. Julián Contreras plays both violin and guitar, which may account for much of his ability to provide fine guitar accompaniment. It is interesting to note that he plays the chord changes with modulating connecting passages to provide a musical framework for the *violinista*. He also anticipates when the *violinista* changes key. New Mexican Hispano folk music is extremely flexible, and musical passages may be performed any number of times before launching into the next. The relationship between the performing musicians is critical and is based on a level of shared consciousness. In the performance of jazz, which highlights improvisation within a given musical structure, the shared level of consciousness, or "musical telepathy," is essential.

La polka Ester has been popular in the Las Cruces area of southern New Mexico around Las Cruces for many years. The version included here was performed by Ventura Rael on violin and Julián Contreras on guitar. At the time it was recorded, Señor Contreras happened to be visiting Señor Rael. Over the years they had performed together only infrequently. Señor Contreras borrowed Señor Rael's guitar, they tuned their instruments, and this spontaneous version of *La polka Ester* resulted. Señor Contreras lives in Hill, New Mexico near the banks of the Río Grande.

La polka Ester

Performed by Ventura Rael y Julián Contreras

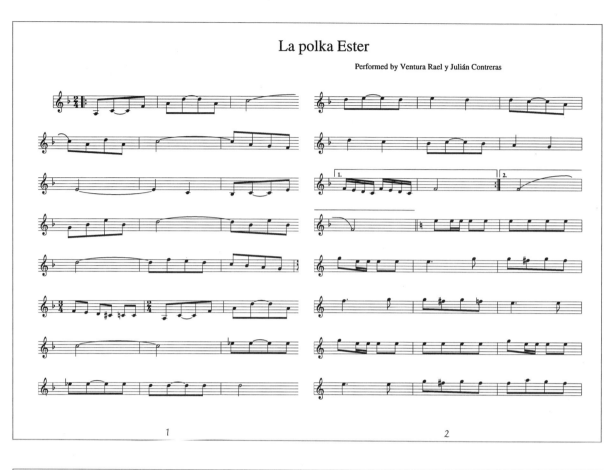

1   2

3   4

(Continued on next page)

La polka Ester

(continued)

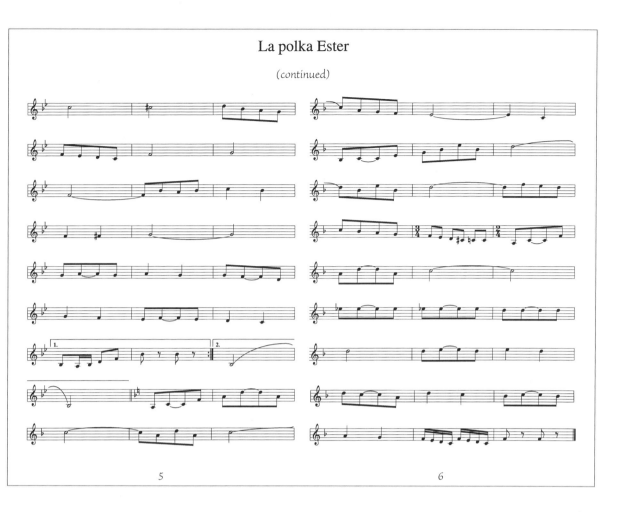

5

6

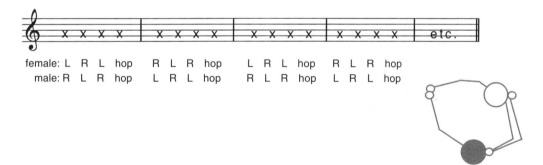

| female: | L R L hop | R L R hop | L R L hop | R L R hop |
| male: | R L R hop | L R L hop | R L R hop | L R L hop |

*O*ne of the most popular songs in the region of the Río Grande del Norte is entitled *Jesusita en Chihuahua,* composed by Quirino Mendoza, father of Lydia Mendoza, the great singer. This polka is perhaps the best current example of a popular song that has become incorporated into the folk repertoire. Over the years we have recorded thirty versions of this melody. In Mexico it is performed by *mariachis* and frequently features trumpets. North of the border, it is often performed by *violinistas* to demonstrate their level of performance skill. It is a polka beloved by all *la gente.*

It should be noted that reading the score of a composition while it is being performed by an instrumentalist who is also reading the score differs from reading the transcription of a performance while listening to the same melody played by the musician from memory. The spontaneity and variable intonation cannot always be perfectly transcribed in Western musical notation.

This version of *Jesusita en Chihuahua* was performed by Ventura Rael, who plays unaccompanied. The musical transcription is intended to be a more or less accurate version of Señor Rael's performance of the melody in his own style. His use of double stops, ornamentation, and pizzicato make it as fine a performance of this polka on violin as we have heard among Hispano folk musicians.

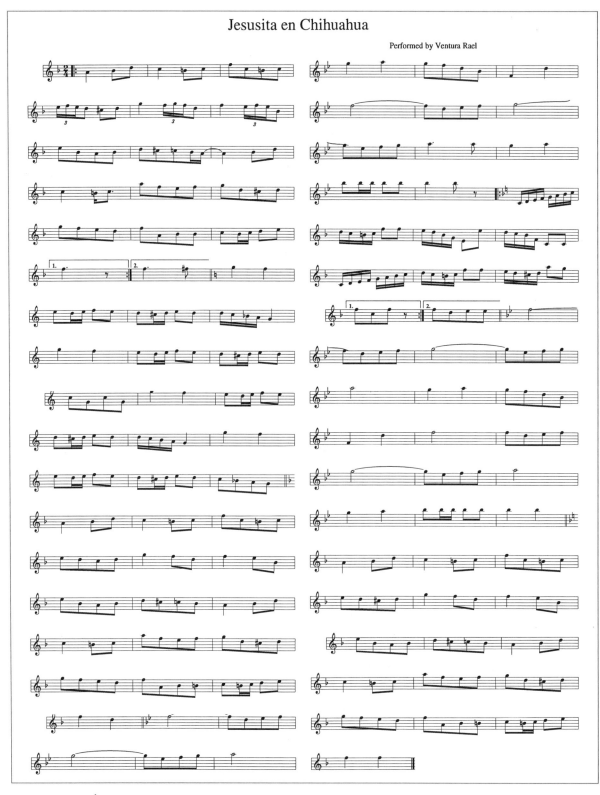

Jesusita en Chihuahua

Performed by Ventura Rael

The town of Ratón lies in the northeast corner of New Mexico, near the headwaters of the Canadian River, which is part of the Arkansas River watershed, the waters of which flow into the Mississippi River. Ratón was originally a mining town that has lured people of different ethnic heritages so that the meld is sometimes apparent in the music. *La polka Pasqualina* is such an example. Señor Lewis Martínez first learned this polka from an Italian friend and incorporated it into his own repertoire.

Señor Martínez is an energetic *violinista*. He was accompanied by his old friend Louis Olguín in the rendition of *La polka Pasqualina* presented here.

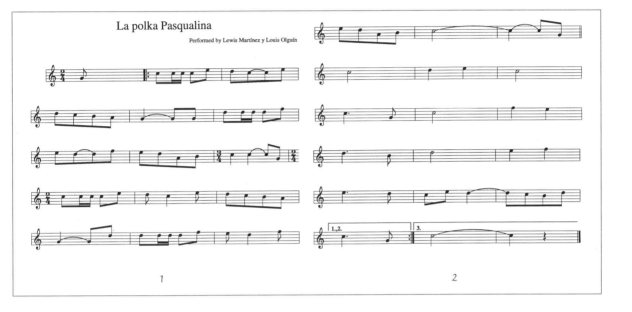

One of the most intricate and interesting of the folk dances performed in the region of the Río Grande del Norte is *La cuna,* the cradle dance. The origins of this dance are difficult to ascertain. Rubén Cobos defines it as a folk dance of New Mexico and southern Colorado. None of the definitions of *cuna* in the *Diccionario Velásquez* refers to a dance form known as such. Inasmuch as this dictionary defines peninsular Spanish, one might conjecture that *La cuna* may be a form known only in the New World. Neither Aurora Lucero-White nor Mela Sedillo de Koeber, two of the principal authorities on New Mexican Hispano folk dance of this century indicates the provenance of *La cuna* in their publications.

La cuna is danced in duple time. It involves groups of two couples facing each other, the women opposite the men. As the dance begins, the women walk forward and grasp the left hands of the men opposite them, as in a handshake. The men turn backward, passing under the elevated left arms of the women. Each woman then grasps the right hand of her own partner in her right hand, making a quarter turn to the left under her partner's arm. All four face forward, still grasping hands, their now intertwined arms forming the *cuna,* or cradle. They dance a two-step in this position, making a rocking motion with their arms, the whole human cluster slowly rotating counterclockwise. All these moves fit within the sixteen measures of the A part of the melody. Throughout the sixteen measures of the B part, the individual couples dance the polka in ballroom position. As the musicians return to part A, the couples again form clusters of four, and the whole process is repeated. *La cuna* requires a lot of practice; otherwise the cradle will fall, along with the dancers, decorum and all. There seems to be at least one variation in the performance of *La cuna,* since the procedure described above differs slightly from that described by Aurora Lucero-White.

In 1617 Fray Pedro de Miranda constructed a mission north of Santa Fe, near the Indian pueblo initially known to the Spaniards as Braba. The pueblo was multistoried and comprised of two structures separated by a creek that streamed southwestward out of the mountains. Spanish settlers moved into the area, but in 1680 they were either killed or forced to flee the wrath of Indians in revolt. In 1692 the Spanish colonists returned and have remained since that time. Their settlement became known as Fernando de Taos. In subsequent decades Taos became a trade center in the north country where Indians of varying lineage bartered among themselves and with descendants of Europeans, both Spanish and French. Sometime after 1820 Anglo mountain men and fur trappers were seen in Taos, and thus people of several cultures passed in and out of each other's wakes.

In the final decade of the nineteenth century, artists and writers discovered that Taos provided an ambiance that set creative forces in motion. To this day people with refined aesthetic sensibilities regard Taos as a place of extraordinary beauty.

Some of New Mexico's finest and most knowledgeable folk musicians have lived in and around Taos. The four individuals who comprised the group known as *Los Alegres* made concerted efforts to perform and preserve Hispano folk music and dance. Two members of that group, José Damián Archuleta and Pablo Trujillo performed the music for the cradle dance entitled *La cuna brava* that is presented here.

La cuna brava

Performed by José Archuleta y Pablo Trujillo

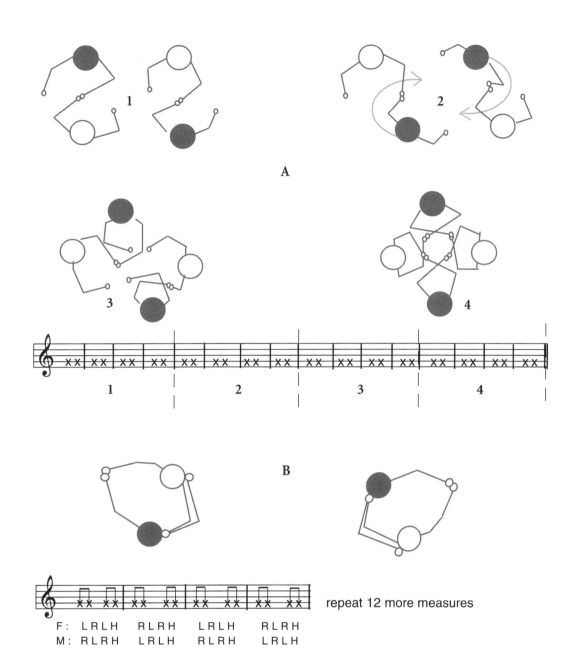

A

B

repeat 12 more measures

F: L R L H   R L R H   L R L H   R L R H
M: R L R H   L R L H   R L R H   L R L H

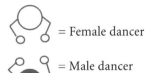 = Female dancer

= Male dancer

Dance positions are keyed to
music on facing and following
pages.

= direction of movement

Jenny Wells Vincent is an Anglo folk musician who has seriously studied Hispano folk music for over fifty years; as a collector she has produced albums of Hispano folk musicians. Mrs. Vincent sings and performs on the accordion. The *Trío de Taos*, which included Jenny Vincent, Hattie Trujillo, and Nat Flores was regarded as one of the best musical groups in New Mexico. They performed the version of *La cuna* presented below which also appears on their album, *Música para una Fiesta*.

La cuna

Performed by Jenny Vincent, Hattie Trujillo y Nat Flores

An area that remained relatively uninhabited by people of Spanish descent until the nineteenth century was the desolate landscape that extends from Las Cruces northward to Socorro. The presence of hostile Apaches and extreme aridity discouraged colonization for generations. The Río Grande meanders through the northern reaches of the Chihuahuan Desert past ranges of mountains separated by deep arroyos that sometimes rage with flash floods. To this day the lands to the east of the river are called La Jornada del Muerto because of the scarcity of water that threatened travelers along this famous shortcut of the Camino Real.

Fifty miles north of El Paso del Norte and west of the Río Grande are the Robledo Mountains. In 1598 as Juan de Oñate led his band of colonists northward, one of his lieutenants, Pedro Robledo, passed from this world at the base of a mountain near a ford across the river. Robledo's mortal remains were buried there and the range immortalizes his name. South of Robledo Peak, to the east of the river, is a snaggle-peaked range now known as the Organ Mountains. In the early nineteenth century, the human remains of Hispanos allegedly massacred by hostile Apaches were found between the base of these mountains and the Río Grande. The mutilated bodies were buried and crosses were mounted to mark the graves. The place of the crosses is known to this day as Las Cruces, New Mexico, and lies in the heartland of the Mesilla Valley, which has become a significant agricultural center in spite of the sparse rainfall. Indeed a torrent of humanity has burst into the valley that until recently resounded only with the echoes of emptiness. Today Las Cruces is the third largest city in New Mexico. Many traditional Hispano folk musicians live in the area and perform music that is also known in Mexico.

The dance known as *La Camila* has been popular from Las Cruces to the San Luis Valley for many years; the name suggests French origin. The melody is still popular among the elderly *gente* of the Río Grande del Norte, but few recall how to perform the dance even though it is relatively simple. The couples either stand facing each other or assume ballroom position. The melody is in 2/4 time and sixteen measures long, with A and B sections of eight measures each. To the first four measures, a couple takes four long steps to the man's left. The man steps sideways with his left foot, sliding his right foot over to meet it. The woman begins with her right foot. To the second four measures, the couple takes eight short steps back to the original position, the man starting with his right foot, the woman with her left. For the remaining eight measures the couple dances a polka or two-step. The entire procedure is repeated again and again until the *músicos* finish playing.

The version of *La Camila* presented here was performed by Pete Maese on the violin and Felix Vega on the guitar, both of whom were recorded in the Maese home in Las Cruces. Señor Maese was born in 1899 and for many years was regarded as one of Las Cruces's leading musicians. He performed the *Matachines* music at Las Tortugas for fifty years. They performed this same version of *La Camila* in the documentary film, *La Música de los Viejos*.

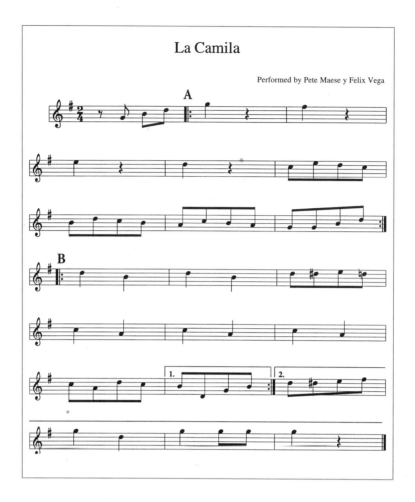

La Camila

Performed by Pete Maese y Felix Vega

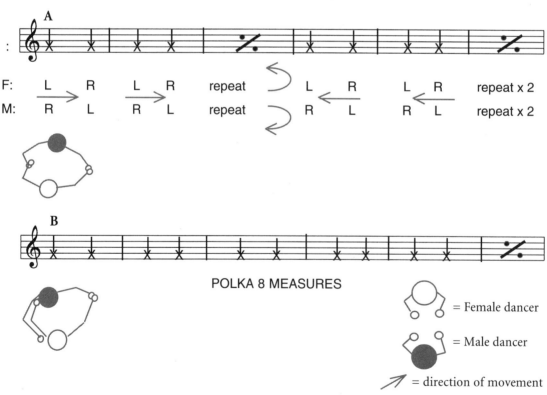

F: L   R   L   R   repeat   L   R   L   R   repeat x 2
M: R   L   R   L   repeat   R   L   R   L   repeat x 2

POLKA 8 MEASURES

= Female dancer

= Male dancer

= direction of movement

A folk dance that is thought to have originated in New Mexico is *El vaquero,* so named because the antics of the dancers suggest the movements of cowboys hopping along in their spurred boots. Many think that this dance reflects the presence of the Gringo cowboy, which established a new archetype in the mythos of American culture, beginning in the latter half of the nineteenth century. According to Helene Mareau, "The steps of this dance savor the rollicking liveliness that American cowboys always inject into their dances." However, as Enrique R. Lamadrid reminds us, cowboys are Americanized *vaqueros.*

The version of *El vaquero* presented here is in 2/4 time. The melody is thirty-two measures long and follows an AA, BB form. The dance involves several couples who face forward, the men to the left of the women, the men holding the women's left hands in their own left hands, and the women's right hands in their own right hands. Each couple advances, skipping on the left foot while holding the right foot up, then stepping forward on the right foot while skipping on the right foot and holding the left foot up, etc. In the sixth measure the dancers take a short step backwards, to dance forward again in the seventh and eighth measures, thus concluding the two A sections. In the B sections, the couple is still holding hands while the woman passes in front of the man, dancing all the way around him in a slow turn. As she approaches his right, she makes a quick full turn so that they are both facing forward again. As she circles him, she completes two counter-clockwise turns. Throughout the man maintains the basic dance step described for section A. This entire procedure is repeated, thus completing the two B sections in sixteen measures, at which point everyone returns to the beginning of the melody and dance. The whole dance is repeated again and again until the *músicos* conclude.

The version of *El vaquero* included here was performed by José Damián Archuleta and Pablo Trujillo of Taos, New Mexico. This dance may be seen in the documentary film *Los Alegres.*

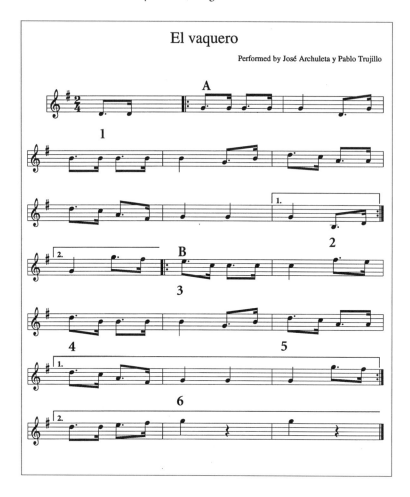

El vaquero

Performed by José Archuleta y Pablo Trujillo

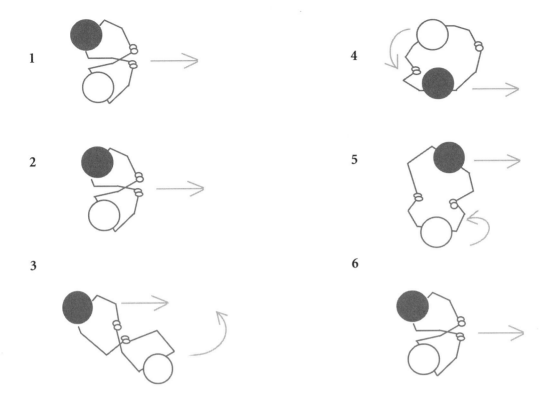

The *chotís* or *chote* is a form of *contredanse* or contra dance that is known in German as the *schottische* which is regarded by many to be what the French call the *écossaise*. Some authorities consider the dance to be of Scottish origin, as the latter two names suggest, whereas others do not. Some believe the dance to be of French origin, conveying the French notion of what a Scottish two-step might be. The origins are admittedly obscure. The schottische is known to have been danced in Britain in 1848, where it was known as the German polka; however, it was not listed by Cellarius in his *La danse des salons*, which was published in Paris in 1847. The *écossaise*, on the other hand, has been known in France from the early eighteenth century. It is possible that these are French and German names for the same dance; both are performed in a fast 2/4 time. An early example of the *écossaise* indicates the melody beginning on the beat, whereas a later schottische shows two sixteenth note pickups at the beginning of the melody.

There are many reports that the schottische was a dance popular in Mexico at the time of Maximilian and that it worked its way northward in that period. However obscure its origin, the *chote* is popular even now among *la gente* of New Mexico and southern Colorado.

The *chote* is a couple dance with A and B sections. In section A, the couples face each other and hold hands. On the first beat of the measure they both dance to the man's right: right-left-right. During the next measure, they dance sideways to the man's left: left-right-left. These sideways shuffling steps are alternated throughout section A. During section B, the couples assume ballroom position and dance a polka step. The entire procedure is repeated until the musicians end the melody.

In the region of the Río Grande del Norte, virtually all of the older *músicos* perform different versions of the *chotís*. The late Macario "Max" Apodaca from Rociada, New Mexico, composed *El chotís Juanito,* which is presented here. Señor Apodaca traveled widely in the West and performed with a group of German musicians in Wyoming. His wife, Antonia, is a spirited and fine guitarist who also plays the accordion, as did her mother, the late Rafelita Martínez (whose music is also included here). The Apodacas were joined in this performance by José Geraldo Martínez of Las Vegas, New Mexico.

El chotís Juanito

Performed by Max y Antonia Apodaca,
y José Geraldo Martínez

Pete Casías was born in 1907 and has spent his life in southern Colorado. For most of his life he performed for traditional dances. He stopped performing in public when his hands fell prey to arthritis, the bane of the performing musician. He nevertheless consented to be recorded in his home in Romeroville, Colorado, performing some of the old pieces he recalled. Among other selections, he performed the complete set of *cuadrillas* mentioned by Aurora Lucero-White, in the order she listed. He was accompanied by his grandson, William Pacheco, on the guitar. Señor Pacheco learned his grandfather's music in order to ensure that within the family, the musical heritage will remain unbroken for at least one more generation.

The following *chote* is entitled *El chotís Ortiz,* which Señor Casías recalled having been performed by a músico named Ortiz many years ago. The A section of the melody line is identical to the A section of the unnamed *chote* played by José Damián Archuleta and Pablo Trujillo in the documentary film *Los Alegres;* the B section is different, however. This is an example of the myriad permutations melodies undergo, as they pass from musician to musician through the generations.

El chotís Ortiz

Performed by Pete Casías y William Pacheco

(Continued on following page)

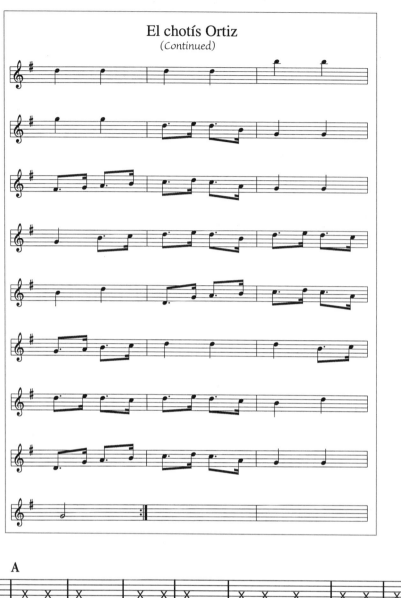

El chotís Ortiz
(Continued)

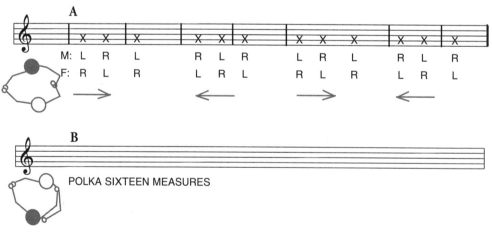

POLKA SIXTEEN MEASURES

The following *chote* was played by Sam Armijo, violin, and Floyd Aguilar, guitar. Señor Armijo works his sheep ranch near Gladstone, New Mexico, and Señor Aguilar worked at the Boys' School in Springer, New Mexico, for twenty-five years before he retired. This particular recording session marked the first time these two *músicos* performed together. Señor Armijo was born in 1914 and Señor Aguilar some thirty years later. Señor Armijo has long been known as a leading fiddler among *la gente* in this sparsely populated and remote area, which extends eastward into the Great Plains. Together these musicians performed a *chote* whose melody has long been familiar but whose name has withered with the passage of the decades.

El chotís

Performed by Sam Armijo y Floyd Aguilar

For the last several decades, folk music has frequently been performed by musicians born outside the culture. This phenomenon, coupled with the advent of media such as radio, phonograph records, audio tape, and now the CD, has made traditional folk music available far beyond its culture of origin. Such musicians have come to be known in certain circles as "revivalists," a designation that should be replaced by something like "resurgents," which is more in keeping with the spirit of the concept. Pete Seeger, the Weavers, and the Kingston Trio are regarded as "revivalists" and have triggered a debate among folklorists and ethnomusicologists that has resulted in a somewhat sticky web. There are those who maintain that "revivalists" steal thunder and "gigs" from "authentic" folk musicians performing the music of their own cultures. There are others who argue that many a folk song would have been relegated to obscurity if it had not been found and performed by a "revivalist." I understand the merits of both arguments but believe that the performance of music cannot be legislated. I would also contend that the presence and commitment of some "resurgents" help prolong the decentralization of popular music performance. By this I mean that the handcrafted quality of folk music is easily differentiated from the electrified, ecclectified aural ambiance of the modern American monoculture stew.

With the advent of serious collectors of folk music who poke their microphones into communities seldom visited by more casual tourists, a sizable body of folk music performed by traditional musicians is available on albums and on the radio. This availability creates its own small havoc among the traditional musicians who had formerly performed solely for the benefit of their respective communities as "culture bearers," in the terminology of the folklorist. In some strange fashion these musicians suddenly become more than they were. Some collectors, myself included, insist on paying musicians for their performance; having been a professional performing musician for many years, I feel it is proper that a musician be adequately compensated. But this changes the context of their performance for many traditional folk musicians. Some traditional folk musicians now perform for recognition outside their cultures and for money, whereas before they performed for the love of it and because it was part of their tradition.

There are some sensitive fieldworkers who legitimately wonder if more harm than good is done by attempting to forestall the inevitable transformation of traditional culture. There are those of us who cannot resist learning to perform the songs we collect, because it gives us tremendous joy and brings joy to others, including the people from whose cultures the music originated.

Jeanie McClerie and Ken Keppeler are fine Anglo musicians who perform both Cajun and Hispano folk music extremely well. They learned much of their *Nuevo mexicano* repertoire from the late Cleofes Ortiz, a traditional *violinista* from Bernal, New Mexico, who was well known throughout the region as one of the greatest musicians of the old-time tradition. One dance tune they learned from Señor Ortiz is *El taleán*, a complicated melody in three parts that is rarely performed correctly, if at all. They learned variations of the dance steps and are currently among the very few who perform this folk dance, the name of which suggests Italian provenance.

In a performance of *El taleán* that took place in Arroyo Seco, New Mexico, the dance involved six couples. The couples stand in two lines, the men on one side, the women on the other. As the A section of the music begins, the first couple holds hands, right hand to right hand, left hand to left. They face the other five couples and dance forward and back, forward and back, until the B section of the music begins. The first couple then squares off with the second couple in the two lines of dancers and they begin to dance the grand right and left, the men grasping the right hands of their respective partners in their own right hands, the men and women then dancing past each other until the men grasp the left hands of the opposite women in their own left hands; thereafter they dance back to their original partners. They then repeat the grand right and left, at which point they reach the C section of the music. Throughout this part the two couples dance the waltz in ballroom position. As the music returns to the A section, the first couple squares off with the third couple, and the entire dance is repeated. By the time the first couple reaches the fourth couple, the second couple squares off with the third couple, and the whole dance evolves to its logical conclusion, each couple having danced *El taleán*.

Helene Mareau describes a variation on this dance that involves only two couples. After the grand right and left, the two couples hold hands in a ring, man-woman-man-woman, the women facing in, the men facing out. The women dance forward and back, while the men dance in position. Thereafter they break and dance another grand right and left, and then once again the two couples hold hands, this time with the men facing in and the women facing out; the men dance forward and back the women dance in position.

The following is the variation that was taught to Jeanie McClerie and Ken Keppeler by Cleofes Ortiz. It was recorded in the living room of my home one wondrous afternoon in the late 1980's. After the recording, the three of us hilariously endeavored to perform the dance with five imaginary partners.

El taleán

Performed by Jeanie McLerie y Ken Keppeler

A

B   Grand right and left two times.

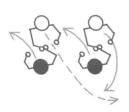

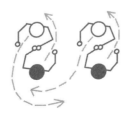

C

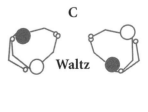

Waltz

Near the southeastern base of the Sangre de Cristo Mountains, where the Río Gallinas flows southward eventually to join the Río Pecos, the settlement of Las Vegas was established in 1835 as the Santa Fe Trail port of entry into Mexico. Eleven years later, Las Vegas came under the control of General Stephen Watts Kearny, who shortly thereafter claimed much of what is now New Mexico for the United States of America. In 1879 a second community was established one mile away from the original when the Santa Fe Railroad depot was constructed. Nearly a century had passed when, in 1970, the two communities became unified under a single city charter.

Las Vegas is an important center of Hispano culture in New Mexico. The architecture in the original community reflects the presence of the past. Spanish is the predominant language, and the mores may be unfamiliar to an outsider. Folk musicians abound in this community, and through their music they remain affiliated with their history. Violins and guitars prevail, and since the turn of the century the button accordion has been played by some musicians.

Santiago Martínez was born in 1904 and performed on the button accordion for many decades. He was one of the most spirited and highly revered *músicos* in old Las Vegas. He would stamp his foot wildly to the rhythm of his playing. His repertoire included many songs from both sides of the current international boundary. *La raspa* is a folk dance that originated in Mexico and is still performed north of the border. Mela Sedillo regards *La raspa* and *Las inditas* to be the same dance; however, the dance steps she describes for *La raspa* do not correspond to the dance steps of *La indita* that I have witnessed and that are described by Aurora Lucero-White.

La raspa is danced by couples who face each other during the A section of the melody. They hold hands and shuffle their feet forward and back to the beat of the music so that when the left foot is forward, the right foot is back. Thinking in terms of the forward foot, then, the dance proceeds left-right-left-rest, right-left-right-rest, etc., throughout the A section of the music. During the B section, the couples assume ballroom position and dance polka-style. The dance is repeated until the musicians stop playing.

The version of *La raspa* presented here was performed by Santiago Martínez on the button accordion. It is in 4/4 time. The A section is eight measures long, and the B section is of four measures. This was recorded in the Martínez home in Las Vegas, New Mexico on August 17, 1978.

La raspa

Performed by Santiago Martínez

In a beautiful mountain valley northwest of Las Vegas beyond Sapelló, where Pablita Ángel murdered her lover, lies the village of Rociada, New Mexico. For many years, Rafelita Martínez lived there and was known throughout the area as one of the foremost musicians. She performed with her late husband, Damasio Martínez. Rafelita was born in 1895, and shortly after the turn of the century she learned to play the button accordion, an instrument only recently arrived in the mountain villages.

The accordion was invented in Europe in the 1820s, having been patented in both Berlin and Vienna. The accordion includes a bellows that forces air around reeds that are selectively activated by depressing buttons or keys, depending on the style of accordion. This instrument is known to have reached northern Mexico by the 1860s. It is possible that it may have accompanied Central European immigrants who settled in the area around San Antonio, Texas, as early as the 1840s. As Manuel Peña points out, the instrument had come into currency by the 1890s as one played at *bailes* in Mexican Texas. And thus it was that the accordion subsequently found its way into the remote corners of Hispano New Mexico.

Señora Martínez passed away in 1981, three years after we recorded her performing several of her favorite melodies. We have included her instrumental version of *La indita,* which is still fondly recalled by many of the elders of the area.

This button accordion version of *La indita* was recorded in Rafelita Martínez's home near Rociada, New Mexico on August 18, 1978.

Una indita

Performed by Rafelita Martínez

In an earlier chapter, *La indita* was described as a narrative ballad akin to the *romance* and the *corrido*. But it is also a form of dance that was common in the region of the Río Grande del Norte until the Second World War. Today the dance is moribund, if it exists at all. Julia Jaramillo of Taos, New Mexico, recalls the basic steps, which she describes as a shuffling polka for couples in AB form. The melody is also in A and B sections, generally of sixteen measures each.

In the A section, facing partners dance in the shuffling polka step in a half circle, forward and back, each keeping to the right of the other. I have seen the women hold both hands at shoulder height, in a style reminiscent of dancing Puebloan women. During this section, the man's hands are either clasped behind his back or simply suspended at his sides. One variation is that the man and woman hold right hands as they dance this section. During the B section, they assume ballroom position and dance the polka shuffle.

The instrumental version of *La indita* included here was performed by the late Cleofes Ortiz, the master *violinista* of Bernal, New Mexico, accompanied on the guitar by his friend Augustine Chávez, from the nearby village of Ribera. Señor Ortiz was born in 1918 and Señor Chávez was born in 1931. This recording was made at the Ortiz home.

La indita

Performed by Cleofes Ortiz y Augustine Chávez

(Continued on next page)

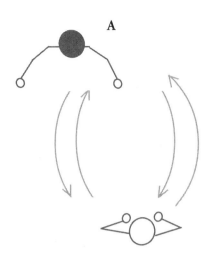

A

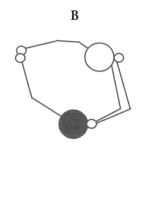

B

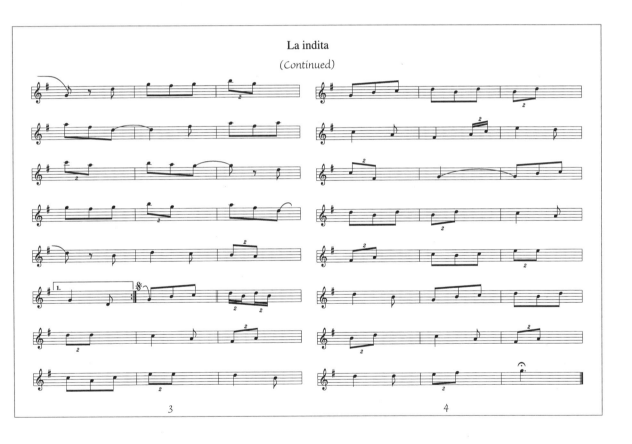

La indita

(Continued)

3

4

The *churrumbé*, is a dance whose origin is obscure; it is apparently known only to a few in northern New Mexico. We have seen it only in Arroyo Seco and are grateful to Julia Jaramillo for having taken the time necessary to help us write it down. Señora Jaramillo pointed out that the *churrumbé* is very similar to the *indita* in form. It involves couples dancing in ballroom position. In the A section the couples first advance in the direction of their outstretched arms according to the following pattern of footwork: left-right, left-right, left-right, left, right, pause. They then back up to their starting point, outstretched arms trailing: right-left, right-left, right-left, right, left, pause. They repeat these moves for the second half of the A section. During the B section, the dancers dance to a polka step.

The rendition of the *churrumbé* presented here was performed by Julia Jaramillo on the mandolin, José Damián Archuleta on the violin, and Pablo Trujillo on the guitar in the Archuleta home in Taos, New Mexico on February 18, 1978.

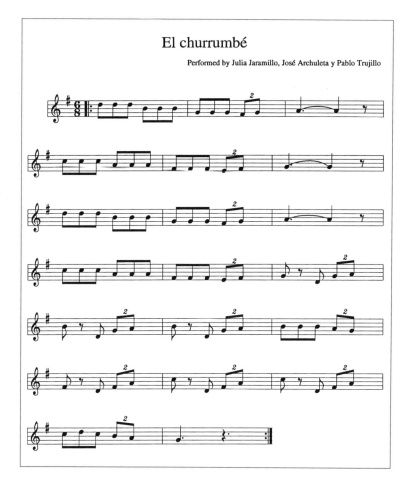

El churrumbé

Performed by Julia Jaramillo, José Archuleta y Pablo Trujillo

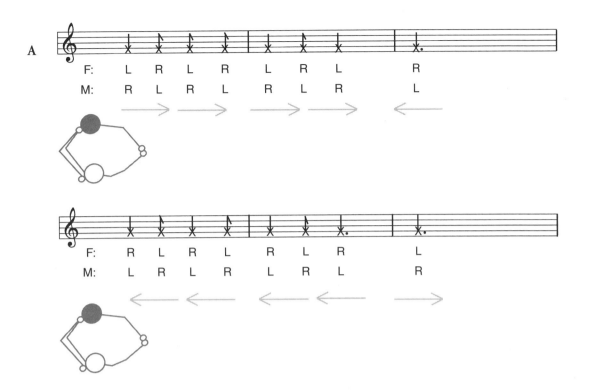

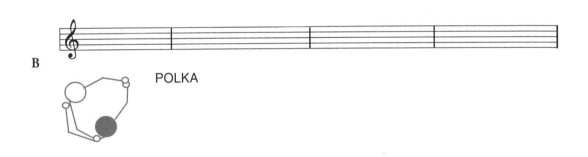

B

POLKA

*L*as cuadrillas is the name that corresponds to a series of folk dances performed by an equal number of couples drawn up in a square. The name comes from the French *quadrille*, which in turn is derived from the Italian word *squadra*. Originally *quadrille* referred not only to dancers but to a squadron of elegantly mounted horsemen numbering from three to fifteen who performed in tournaments. Interestingly the Spanish word *cuadrilla* also refers to a group of four *bandilleros*, the men who stick the darted funeral banners into the neck of the bull in the Spanish bullfight.

The French *quadrille* had assumed its current form by the beginning of the nineteenth century. It then became the prototype of the New England quadrille, which is included in the repertoire of the American square dance. The French version includes a set of five distinct dances: *Le Pantalon*, consisting of thirty-two measures in 6/8 time; *L'Été*, consisting of thirty-two measures in 2/4 time and regarded as a very graceful and difficult contra dance already popular by 1800; *La Poule*, comprised of thirty-two measures in 6/8 time that attained popularity in 1802; a dance consisting of thirty-two measures in 2/4 time in which two figures, *La Trenise* and *La Pastourelle* occur; and the *Finale*, consisting of three parts repeated four times.

The Hispano *cuadrillas* are descended from this French ancestor, which undoubtedly arrived in Mexico by the midnineteenth century. In her publication "Folk Dances of the Spanish Colonials of New Mexico," Aurora Lucero-White lists the six *partes*, or sections, of *Las cuadrillas*, the sixth part being a *cutilio*, or cotillion, which was apparently added after 1848, at the time of the California gold rush and the close of the Mexican–American War.

The six parts of *Las cuadrillas* cited in Lucero-White's description are as follows: *La cuadrilla*, in 2/4 time; *La polka*, in 2/4 time; *La mano derecha*, in 6/8 time; *El galope*, in 6/8 time; *La polka cruzada*, in 2/4 time; and *El cutilio*, in 6/8 time. It should be noted that Eunice Hawkins's transcription of the music for *La cuadrilla* could more appropriately have been transcribed in 6/8 time.

We have recorded many versions of *Las cuadrillas* by different *músicos*, nine of which we analyzed rhythmically. Only one corresponds to the version presented by Lucero-White, and even there the melody for the *cutilio* was performed in 2/4 time. The cotillion is in 3/4 time and was originally a dance popular at the time of Louis XIV. Modern cotillions appear in various fashions and employ waltzes and *mazurkas*, both of which are in triple time, as well as polkas and *galopes*, both of which are in duple time. Furthermore it should be noted that *El galope* cited in Lucero-White is performed in 6/8 time, whereas it is defined in both the *Groves Dictionary of Music and Musicians* and the *Harvard Dictionary of Music* as being in 2/4 time. These details provide some perspective for listening to folk music forms that are called one thing but sound like something else.

Willie Apodaca, who at the time of writing was in his seventies and who for many years was actively involved as a square dancer in Santa Fe, informed me that as a youngster near Las Vegas, New Mexico, he recalled the dance steps of *Las cuadrillas* having been called by a dance caller who spoke in Spanish. The late José Damián Archuleta from Taos, New Mexico, who was one of the best *violinistas* in the region, mentioned that he recalled only the *cutilio* being called, and in English rather than Spanish. It must be borne in mind that New Mexico is nearly two-thirds the size of the country of Spain but with a human population of well under two million, which includes Native Americans, Hispanos, and Anglos. Considering that the Hispano communities are separated by many miles and mountain ranges with peaks of twelve or thirteen thousand feet, it is not surprising that the melodies, musical forms, and order of performance of *Las cuadrillas* in Romeroville, Colorado, may differ from those of Las Cruces, New Mexico.

We have never recorded the actual steps to *Las cuadrillas,* and the music presented here does not precisely correspond to any extant choreography known to us. The presentation of the version of *Las cuadrillas* included in Aurora Lucero-White's book on Spanish Colonial folk dances is excellent. It is also incorporated into Richard Stark's book on the music of New Mexican folk dances.

The version of *Las cuadrillas* included here was performed by Vicente Montoya, violin, and Margarito Olivas, guitar. The late Señor Montoya was one of the greatest folk musicians of his time. He was born blind and developed an extraordinary memory. He performed with equal ease on the violin and twelve-string guitar. He sang in a high tenor voice and recalled many *corridos*. Margarito Olivas has been blind since childhood and still performs with *músicos* in the area around Las Vegas, New Mexico. This was recorded in the home of Margarito Olivas and his mother, Juanita on September 8, 1978.

Las cuadrillas I

Performed by Vicente Montoya & Margarito Olivas

Las cuadrillas II

Performed by Vicente Montoya & Margarito Olivas

Las cuadrillas III

Performed by Vicente Montoya & Margarito Olivas

Las cuadrillas IV

Performed by Vicente Montoya & Margarito Olivas

Las cuadrillas V

Performed by Vicente Montoya & Margarito Olivas

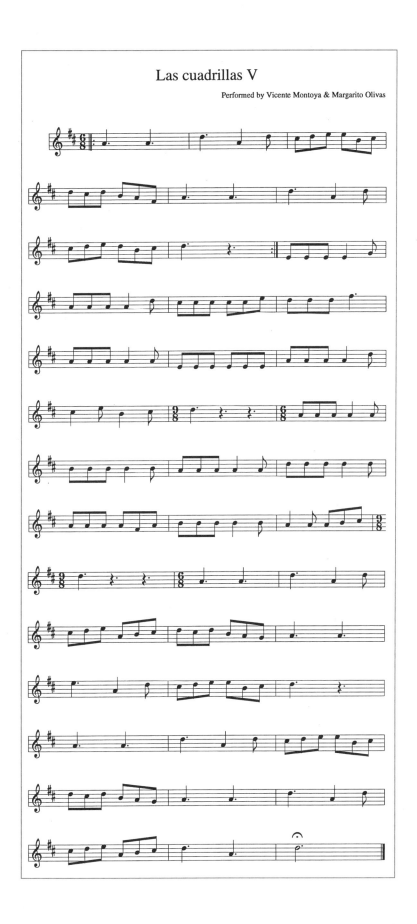

Las cuadrillas VI

Performed by Vicente Montoya & Margarito Olivas

Las cuadrillas VII El cutilio

Performed by Vicente Montoya & Margarito Olivas

CHAPTER SEVEN

Más Cantos, el Teatro, y los Matachines

A S THE PRESSURE OF NORTHERN TRIBES dislodged the grasp of the Roman Empire from the land, Europe entered a period of decentralization pejoratively known as the Dark Ages. For half a millennium, the self-appointed aristocracy contended for control of local areas and subjugated the resident serfs to their will. Men of learning were cloistered in monasteries and conversed and wrote in Latin. The intellectually unsophisticated communicated in local dialects of evolving languages. Cultural evolution slowed to wintry proportions.

By the end of the millennium, the continent was growing ripe for a new burst of human activity, and parts of the human population began expressing themselves in new ways. Poets known as troubadours began inventing verses in the language of the people of southern France (*langue d'oc*) rather than Latin, which persisted as the language of the learned. This region flourished as a cultural entity beginning in the tenth century, producing troubadour literature, Romanesque architecture, the revival of Roman law, and urbanization. Throughout the twelfth and thirteenth centuries, troubadours from southern France and *trouvères* from northern France helped set the stage for the appearance of new poetic forms.

One of the many musical forms thought to have descended from this period is the *trovo*, where two or more people engage in a musical contest, singing alternate *versos* in what Cobos regards as a poetic joust. This poetic dialogue involved a wide range of themes, ranging from philosophical to insulting. The nineteenth century yielded several master *trovadores* whose reputations extended into the twentieth century. These men lived in northern Mexico and New Mexico and thrilled rural audiences with their poetic repartee. Chicoria, El Pelón, Gracia, and El Viejo Vilmas were among the most famous, and some of their *trovos* have been committed to paper, although few, if any, survive within the oral tradition of *la gente*.

Robb's research has revealed that Chicoria hailed from Los Griegos, now part of Albuquerque, while El Pelón was christened Jesús Gonzales and was born in Pojoaque, New Mexico, in 1844. Gracia came from Chihuahua, Mexico. El Viejo Vilmas's past has been obscured by the years, but he was referred to as the insolent New Mexican in a *trovo* cited by Campa.

Even though the burst of musical and poetic energy that resulted in the *trovo* now casts only the dimmest of shadows in today's world, one has found its way into the present collection. It was recollected by Cipriano Vigil, who originally heard it as a youth in Chamisal, New Mexico. He was joined by Enrique R. Lamadrid in the performance of *El trovo del Viejo Dimas y Gracia,* two of the above-mentioned *trovadores.* In this rendition, El Viejo is known as Dimas, a transmutation of the name Vilmas. Part of this *trovo* appears in a longer form in Robb's opus.

El trovo del Viejo Dimas y Gracia

Enrique R. Lamadrid & Cipriano Vigíl

Gracia:
Maestro Dimas, ¿dónde estás
entre semanas y días?
Que te han salido a buscar
más de cuatro compañías
y no te han podido hallar
entre semanas y días.

Maestro Dimas:
Nulas son tus fantasías
te acabo de noticiar.
¿Dónde son tus compañías
que me han salido a buscar
que no me han podido hallar
entre semanas y días?

Gracia:
Por la flor de Alejandría
breve lo pondré en mi lista.
Maestro Dimas lo menor,
el que era de Buena Vista.

Maestro Dimas:
También te pondré en mi conquista
para que puedas dishurgar.
Me han dicho que tú eres Gracia,
conmigo no has de jugar.

Gracia:
Maestro, se tiene que dar
como tierra de verano.
¿Qué tal chuliarían a Gracia
si le ganaba un anciano?

Maestro Dimas:
Torpe estás como el gusano,
te acabo de competir.
Yo también canto lozano,
no me has de contradecir.

Trovo of Dimas the Elder and Gracia

Enrique R. Lamadrid & Cipriano Vigíl

Gracia:

Master Dimas, where have you been
these weeks and days?
For more than four companies
have gone out looking for you
and have not found you
all these weeks and days.

Dimas the Elder:
Your fantasies are null,
I have just told you.
Where are your companies
that have gone to look for me
and haven't been able to find me
all these weeks and days?

Gracia:
By the flower of Alexandria
I will soon have you on my list.
Maestro Dimas the least,
is he that was from Buena Vista.

Dimas the Elder:
I will add you to my conquests
so that you may amuse us.
They have told me you are Gracia
but you won't play around with me.

Gracia:
Maestro, you will have to give way
like the earth of summer.
How would they ridicule Gracia
if an old man beat him?

Dimas the Elder:
You are dull as a worm,
I have already competed with you.
I also sing forcefully
and you will not contradict me.

Gracia:
Maestro, le voy a aplaudir,
mi trovo no tiene taja.
Si alguna plana me enmienda
ni en la tierra queda Gracia.

Maestro Dimas:
Gracia fuere que conmigo
dijiera soy bueno, Gracia,
y en puntito tan teno
cantarás con eficacia.

Gracia:
Breve daremos la traza
pongan el verso refleja.
Maestro, aunque quiera ser bueno
su antigüedad no lo deja.

Maestro Dimas:
De mi voz nadie se queja
de lo dicho a lo vulgar.
Yo soy como el astro sereno
cuando subo a devisar.

Gracia:
Yo soy el Gracia mentado
que ha transitado la aurora.
Yo soy el poeta mentado
que alaban mucho en Sonora.

Maestro Dimas:
Me bajé a la cantimplora
con satisfacción completa
y si no mírame aquí
el Viejo carga paleta.

Gracia:
Mi voz ha sido discreta
y en todo soy victorioso
¿Qué tal chuliarán al viejo
si le ganaba un mocoso?

Maestro Dimas:
Maestro, no se muestre reguroso
que yo canto de noche y día,
ahora quiero que me cantes
textos de filosofía.

Gracia:
Si entiendes filosofía
dale a tu discurso volar.
Para gobierno del cielo
¿qué cosa mi Dios haría?

Gracia:
Maestro, I will applaud you
but my verses have no match.
If any line is surpassed
earth will be no place for Gracia.

Dimas the Elder:
It would be very gracious
if Gracia would admit I am good
and on such a tender point
you will sing effectively.

Gracia:
Soon we shall give contest
let our verses reflect our skill.
Maestro, you may want to be good
but your age will not permit you.

Dimas the Elder:
Nobody complains of my voice
from what is said to what is vulgar
I am like a star serene
when I rise to take a look.

Gracia:
I am the celebrated Gracia
who has traversed the dawn.
I am the celebrated poet
who was much praised in Sonora.

Dimas the Elder:
I went down to the canteen
with complete satisfaction
and if you don't see me here
the Old One carries his stick.

Gracia:
My voice has been discrete
and in all I am victorious
How they would ridicule the old man
if a brat should beat him!

Dimas the Elder:
Maestro, don't seem so bothered
that I can sing day and night,
now I want you to sing me
texts of philosophy.

Gracia:
If you understand philosophy
give wings to your speech.
In the government of Heaven
what would my God do?

Maestro Dimas:
Cuando su muerte notoria
de esa ciudad solomada
dice la sagrada historia,
¿en qué modo fue formada?

Gracia:
¿En qué modo fue formada?
ahora les pregunto yo,
¿Cuáles son los querubines
que un serafín algo goza?

Maestro Dimas:
¿Acuál es la estrella más hermosa
que al mundo dé claridad?
¿Qué título se da a los jardines,
ahora les pregunto yo?

Gracia:
Ahora les pregunto yo
poetas y compositores,
¿cuántos fueron los colores
que Dios a la Gloria dio
cuántos jardines plantó?

Maestro Dimas:
¿Más esencial, cuál es el río
de Jordán donde se paseó María?
Dale a tu discurso vuelo
si entiendes filosofía,
para gobierno del cielo
¿qué cosa mi Dios haría?

Dimas the Elder:
When his notorious death
in that singular city
the sacred story tells,
how was it formed?

Gracia:
How was it formed
I ask you now.
Which are the cherubim
that a seraphim enjoys?

Dimas the Elder:
Which is the most beautiful star
that gives clarity to the world?
What title is given to the gardens,
I ask you now?

Gracia:
Now I ask you,
poets and composers,
how many were the colors
that God gave to Heaven,
how many gardens did He plant?

Dimas the Elder:
More essential, which is the river
Jordan where Mary walked?
Give wings to your speech
if you understand philosophy,
in the government of Heaven
what would my God do?

El trovo del Viejo Dimas y Gracia

Performed by Enrique R. Lamadrid y Cipriano Vigil

In addition to the *indita* (see chapter 3), another musical form found almost exclusively in New Mexico is the *cuando;* neither form is presently heard very frequently. Robb lists three *cuandos* in his great work, two of which he recorded, the third having been recorded by Rubén Cobos. According to both Robb and Cobos, *cuandos* are songs where each stanza ends with the word *cuando* ("when"). Some *cuandos* appear with texts of eight-line stanzas, whereas others employ *décimas,* or ten-line stanzas. Only two *cuandos* appear in our collection to date, both of which were performed by Cipriano Vigil, who learned them as a boy from an elderly neighbor in Chamisal, New Mexico. Both of these *cuandos* are in *décima* form; however, they differ from those described above in that the word *cuando* comes at the beginning of each stanza rather than at the end.

The example here is entitled *Cuando de los cazadores* and is thought by Señor Vigil to have been composed in the first half of the nineteenth century. The subject matter certainly indicates that the song corresponds to a time when *la gente* relied on their hunting abilities for both food and clothing. This ballad illustrates a long-vanished point of view and thus lends emphasis to the notion that folk music is capable of resurrecting a sense of forgotten ethos, if only for a few moments.

Cuando de los cazadores

Cipriano Vigil

¡Qué destino tan carajo
tienen ya los cazadores!
No alcanzan para camisa
ni más para calzones.

Cuando se cargan sus balas
de pólvora suda el brazo,
cuando vienen de cazar
vienen a darles un asco.
Cuando estudian pa' contar
diciendo fue jacalos,
se lo metí al corazón
echó sangre y también pelos.
Luego se van por los probes,
¡Qué destino tan carajo!

Con las garras del sombrero
y la falda ariscadita
cuando pasan días enteros
mirando las pisaditas.
Deseando siquiera ver
también le echan borrones
pensando que son venados
le tiran a los troncones.

The Hunters

Cipriano Vigil

What a hell of a fate
have the hunters!
They can't even afford
a shirt let alone pants.

When they load their bullets
with gunpowder their arms sweat,
when they come from hunting
they are really disgusting.
When they study how to count
saying, it was luck
I got him through the heart
blood and hair all over.
Then they go among the poor,
what a hell of a fate!

With rags for a hat
and their skirts gathered
when they pass whole days
looking for tracks.
Wanting at least to see
shadows come over
thinking they are deer
they shoot at trees.

Pero cómo están salados
no alcanzan ni pa' calzones.

Cuando llegan a tirar
no más se les van heridos
ya no les sirve ni el cuero
cuando los hayan perdidos.
Reciben gran desconsuelo
por haber sido de los mejores
por no haber sido saurín
se tomó por estos soles.
Señores, pos, este fin
tienen los cazadores.

Cuando se usa
camita de era
no alcanzan perdón de Dios
no faltando la primera
solo de hambre mata a dos.
Se tiran por la ladera
sin pronunciar más razón
matan uno por adentro
cazándolos como león,
no alcanzan pa' bastimiento
conti' más para calzón.

But how unlucky they are
they can't even afford pants.

When they finally get a shot
the game gets away injured
not even the hide is good
when they find the lost ones.
They receive great grief
having been some of the best
for not having been around
they were taken for suns.
People, well, this is the fate
of the hunters

When they use
a bed on the ground
they are not pardoned by God,
in lacking one for hunger
two are killed.
They shoot on the mountainside
without pronouncement of reason
they kill their game far away
hunting like lions, they don't
even get enough to put away,
not to mention their pants.

Cuando de los cazadores

Performed by Cipriano Vigil

Until recent times, the *décima* enjoyed immense popularity throughout the region of the Río Grande del Norte. Although it is still viable in the Caribbean and parts of South America, the form has all but disappeared from the *Nuevo Mexicano* repertory. It can be traced to fifteenth-century Spain. As a literary form it is thematically linked to virtually every aspect of Hispano culture. Traditionally the *décima* contains forty-four lines. It begins with a *planta*, or introductory stanza of four octosyllabic lines, followed by four stanzas of ten octosyllabic lines—hence the term *décima*. Aurelio Espinosa regarded this form as " … one of the outstanding examples of the persistence of Spanish tradition in New Mexico." There are *décimas* of New Mexican origin that follow the form invented in Spain.

The ten-line stanzas assumed the somewhat fixed rhyme pattern *abbaaccddc,* called an *espinela* after the Spaniard Vincent Espinel, who is thought by some but certainly not by all to have introduced it. Señor Espinel was a renowned composer and guitarist who was also a poet, novelist, soldier, vagabond, and priest. He was born in Ronda and died in Madrid in 1624.

Although it prevailed as a poetic and musical form for so long, the *décima* is now all but extinct in the Río Grande del Norte. Robb has written an enlightening chapter regarding this form and has included twenty-nine different texts. He points out that the melodies are generally variations on the same theme and share "a sort of modal ambiguity."

In 1963 Robb recorded a *décima* in Galisteo, New Mexico, entitled *El huérfano,* for which he included no musical transcription. It also lacks the four-line introductory planta. In La Mesa, New Mexico, we recorded a song of the same title to a melody that totally differs from those presented by Robb. However, by comparing the lyrics, one can determine that they are versions of the same *décima.*

A rendition of *El huérfano* similar in text and melody appears in Paredes's *Cancionero.* Paredes points out that this song combines the literary form of the *décima* with the musical form of the *corrido.* He also notes that *El huérfano* is the type of song sometimes referred to as a *canción de ciego,* meaning that it may be sung by blind beggars in Mexico who make their livelihood by singing for beneficent passersby. *El huérfano* is truly a poignant song both lyrically and melodically. The version presented here was performed by Claudio Sáenz of La Mesa, New Mexico, who learned the song from Mexican musicians.

El huérfano

Claudio Sáenz

Pues yo pienso y me confundo,
es muy cierto y muy notable,
la gran desdicha en el mundo
no tener uno a sus padres.
Como la pluma en el aire,
anda el hijo ya perdido,
el huérfano desvalido
pierde la honra y el decoro.
Óigame, mis amigos,
estas lágrimas que lloro.

The Orphan

Claudio Sáenz

Well, I think and am confused,
it is quite certain and notable,
the great disgrace in this world
is not having your parents.
Like a feather in the wind,
the lost child wanders,
the destitute orphan
loses honor and decorum.
Listen, my friends,
to these tears I cry.

Estas lágrimas que lloro	These tears I cry
no las lloro de cobarde,	are not out of cowardice,
las lloro porque me acuerdo	I cry them because I remember
de los consejos de mi madre.	the advice of my mother.
Unas veces de soldado,	Sometimes as a soldier,
otras veces en prisiones,	other times in prisons,
mi padre atribulado,	my father in tribulation,
mi madre con aflicciones,	my mother with afflictions,
me llenaban de oraciones	they filled me with prayers,
cuando yo encuerda salía.	when I would leave with my hands bound.
Y mi madre el alma mía,	And my mother, my soul,
lloraba por mí en la calle,	cried for me in the street,
así mi suerte sería	thus would be my luck
hoy que reflección es tarde.	now that reflection comes too late.
Para el huérfano no hay sol,	For the orphan there is no sun,
ya no hay lluvia, no hay nevada.	there is no rain, there is no snow.
Todos le hacen mala cara	Everyone scorns him,
ni superando el dolor,	not overcoming the pain,
ni quien le haga un favor,	with nobody to do him a favor,
todos a él muestran tiranos.	everyone shows him their tyranny.
Parientes, primos y hermanos	Relatives, cousins, and brothers
lo avergüenzan en la calle,	shame him in the streets,
a cada paso que doy,	with every step I take,
son recuerdos de mi madre.	are the memories of my mother.
Pobrecita de mi madre	My poor mother,
con qué lástima murió,	what a shame that she died.
Ahora sí ya se quedó	Now she will remain
en el sueño más profundo.	in the deepest sleep.
Pero desgraciado yo,	And I am the one disgraced,
que quedé solo en el mundo.	remaining alone in the world.
Del cielo cayó una flor	A flower fell from the sky
en el viento la capié.	and in the wind I caught it in my cape.
Del cielo cayó una flor	A flower fell from the sky
en el viento la capié.	and was stripped by the wind.
A toditos mis amigos	To all of my friends,
el huérfano les canté.	the orphan has sung.
A toditos mis amigos	To all of my friends,
el huérfano les canté.	the orphan has sung.

El huérfano

Performed by Claudio Sáenz

In the *Nuevo Mexicano* communities of the Río Grande del Norte, there is a lively and colorful repertory of religious and secular folk plays that are performed on plazas and in churches for feast days across the region. The colonization of New Mexico began with a play. On April 30, 1598, as soon as the colonists led by Don Juan de Oñate crossed the Río Grande into New Mexico, North America's first Thanksgiving feast was held. The celebration was accompanied by "*Juegos de moros y cristianos,*" a medieval folk play featuring wild horseplay and pitched battles between Christians and Moors. The secular repertory that developed over the coming centuries also includes "Los comanches" and "Los tejanos," which celebrate victories over Indian and Anglo-Texan foes. Both "Moros y cristianos" and "Los comanches" can be seen regularly in the northern New Mexico villages of Chimayó and Alcalde.

The religious repertory is more extensive, featuring a cycle of *autos,* or morality plays, on a series of topics, including "Adán y Eva" ("Adam and Eve"), "Las cuatro apariciones de Guadalupe" ("The Four Apparitions of Guadalupe"), "Los pastores" ("The Shepherds"), "El niño perdido" ("The Lost Child"), and the Nativity play entitled "Los comanches," among others. Many of the plays feature music and singing that is as unique and beautiful as anything else in the regional folk repertory. Most of these plays are only rarely performed. "Los pastores," or the Christmas shepherds' play, can be seen in season almost anywhere in the region, from the San Luis Valley in the north to Las Cruces in the south. "Los comanches" is also enjoying a revival after a lengthy period of dormancy. Thanks to the efforts of directors such as Larry Torres of Arroyo Seco and folklorist Enrique R. Lamadrid, the plays are being appreciated by a public just beginning to discover its folk roots. Our collection is a brief sampler of the music of three of the most popular plays.

When the Spanish colonists returned to the Río Grande del Norte in 1692 after the Pueblo Revolt of 1680, the great *mestizaje,* or mixture, of bloodlines and cultural elements between Spanish and Puebloan peoples began in earnest. However, the mantle of peace was not to settle over the land for another century. Navajos and Apaches raided the *pueblos* and *placitas* of the valleys, exacting their own tribute and vengeance and punishing incursions into their realms. Bursting upon the scene in the first years of the eighteenth century, the Comanche Indians soon became the sworn enemies of the Spanish colonists and their Puebloan neighbors. When provoked they attacked with a relentless and terrifying ferocity. Once they acquired horses and firearms, they were as formidable a fighting force as anything the colonial government could muster.

Aurelio Espinosa cited an early eighteenth-century observer who noted that "Their only idols are freedom and war …" The great chief Cuerno Verde boasted that he could obliterate New Mexico any time he wanted; he just needed some *Nuevo Mexicanos* and Pueblo Indians to raise his horses and corn for him. Campaign after military campaign was mounted but only resulted in a deadlier web of revenge. Finally Governor de Anza put together a huge army of militia men, Pueblo auxiliaries, and Ute allies to decisively defeat Cuerno Verde in southern Colorado in the summer of 1779.

In celebration of the end of hostilities and the beginning of a lasting peace, a historical folk drama known as "Los comanches" emerged that is still performed to this day. Enrique R. Lamadrid has conducted extensive research on and field recordings of "Los comanches," including the verse that introduces the *arenga,* or harangue, by Cuerno Verde, preceded and followed by the vocable singing of Hispano Comanche music.

Singer Francisco "el Comanche" Gonzales remembers the folk drama clearly, since he played the part of a captive child in it. Today "Los comanches" can be seen only in Alcalde, New Mexico, where mounted Spanish soldiers and Comanche warriors taunt and fight each other.

Arenga de Cuerno Verde

Francisco Gonzales

Del oriente al poniente,
del sur al norte frío,
suenen brillantes clarines,
y brille el acero mío.

Cuerno Verde's Harangue

Francisco Gonzales

From the east to the west,
from the south to the cold north,
may brilliant trumpets blare
and my steel shine.

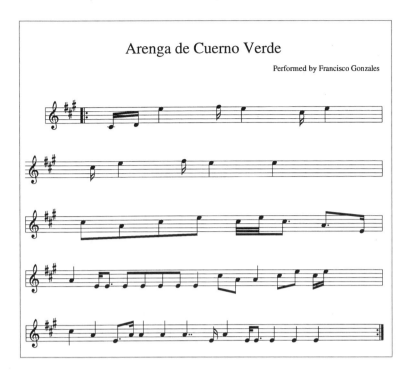

Arenga de Cuerno Verde

Performed by Francisco Gonzales

Another manifestation of the regional Comanches celebrations is a Nativity play, also called "Los comanches," from western New Mexico, where the Christ Child is visited and kidnapped by villagers garbed as Comanche Indians. He is ransomed and returned unscathed. Part of the drama includes a song sung by a chorus of Comanches who come to dance for the Santo Niño. The verses of the song are sung in Spanish and the chorus in vocables, to evoke the Native American presence.

This song is an example of the intercultural exchange that took place in the eighteenth and nineteenth centuries between the peoples of the Río Grande del Norte. In Bernalillo, New Mexico, it is performed in church on Christmas Eve by a large group of children dressed in buckskin and feathers. Here, *Los comanchitos* is performed in a concert setting by Brenda Romero, Enrique R. Lamadrid, Chuy Martínez, and Cipriano Vigil.

Los comanchitos

Brenda Romero, Enrique R. Lamadrid, Chuy Martínez, and Cipriano Vigil

Aquí estoy, Santo Niñito
para cumplir mi promesa,
este grupo de comanchitos
me vienen a acompañar.

En el marco de esta puerta
pongo un pie, pongo los dos,
a toditita esta gente,
buenas noches les dé Dios.

The Little Comanches

Brenda Romero, Enrique R. Lamadrid, Chuy Martínez, and Cipriano Vigil

Here I am, Holy Child,
to fulfill my promise,
this group of little Comanches
comes to accompany me.

In the threshold of this door,
I put one foot, I put both,
to all of these people,
may God give you a good night.

A mí no me lleva el río
por muy crecido que vaya,
y yo sí me llevo al Niño
con una buena bailada.

coro:
Ana, jeyana, jeyana, jeyó,
ana, jeyana, jeyana, jeyó,
anayana yo, anayana yo,
anayana yo, anayana yo,
ana, jeyana, jeyana, jeyó,
ana, jeyana, jeyana, jeyó.

Niño lindo, Manuelito,
tú solito no más sabes
el corazón de cada uno,
también sus necesidades.

Esta noche es Noche Buena,
noche de comer buñuelos,
en mi casa no los hay
por falta de harina y huevo.

Nos despidimos de todos,
de todos en cambullón,
les deseamos felicidades
por su buena atención.

Al Santo Niño de Atocha
le encargamos por favor,
cuide de sus comanchitos
que no olvide cuántos son.

coro

The river won't take me,
no matter how high its flood,
I'll take the Child along
with a good dance.

chorus:
Ana, heyana, heyana, heyo,
ana, heyana, heyana, heyo,
anayana yo, anayana yo,
anayana yo, anayana yo,
ana, heyana, heyana, heyo,
ana, heyana, heyana, heyo.

Beautiful Child, little Emmanuel,
only you can know
the heart of each one,
and also its needs.

Tonight is Christmas Eve,
the night to eat fried bread,
at my house we have none
because there is no flour or eggs.

We take our leave of all,
of all in a group,
we wish you happiness
for all your attentions.

To the Holy Child of Atocha,
we entrust you please,
take care of your little Comanches,
don't forget how many there are.

chorus

Los comanchitos

Performed by Brenda Romero, Enrique Lamadrid,
Cipriano Vigil y Chuy Martinez

One of the most poignant of the *Nuevo Mexicano* folk dramas of the Río Grande del Norte is "Los pastores," a play which features *borregueros,* or shepherds, who are guided by a brilliant star to the birthplace of the Christ Child. Depending on the version being performed, the cast includes the shepherds Bato, Bartolo (who is lazy and self-indulgent), Tetuán, Tubal, Tebano, and Lipio; Arcángel Miguel; Ermitaño, Lucifer, and the beautiful young shepherdess, Gilita. The shepherds are journeying to *Belén,* or Bethlehem, to present gifts to the Christ Child. They encounter a hermit along the way who accompanies them. Unfortunately Lucifer has noticed their pilgrimage and does everything in his power to divert it. He tempts the shepherds and the hermit, but San Miguel comes to the rescue with his sword and defeats the dark angel.

During the course of their journey, Gilita sings two beautiful songs that express her love of the Santo Niño: *Camina, Gilita,* and *A la rú.*

Camina, Gilita and A la rú are lullabies that have been known and sung in every *Nuevo Mexicano* household with an infant. Here the songs are performed by Brenda Romero, a New Mexican folksinger and folkdancer who was raised in Lyden, New Mexico, and who is a professor of ethnomusicology at the University of Colorado.

Camina, Gilita

Brenda Romero

Camina, Gilita,
que vendrás cansada,
ya mero llegamos
a nuestra posada.
Ya mero llegamos
a nuestra posada.

Las estrellas tiemblan
y luego se paran,
absortas se quedan
de tanta nevada.
Absortas se quedan
de tanta nevada.

Voy para Belén
con gusto infinito,
A llevarle al Niño
este pañalito.
A llevarle al Niño
este pañalito.

Walk, Gilita

Brenda Romero

Walk on, Gilita,
you must be tired,
soon we'll arrive
at our resting place.
Soon we'll arrive
at our resting place.

The stars tremble
and later pause
in amazement
with so much snow.
They are amazed
with so much snow.

I'm going to Bethlehem
with infinite joy,
to take the Child
this little diaper.
To take the Child
this little diaper.

Camina, Gilita

Performed by Brenda Romero

A la rú

Brenda Romero

Duérmete, Niño lindo,
en los brazos del amor,
mientras que duerme y descansa,
la pena de mi dolor.

A la rú, a la me
a la rú, a la me,
a la rú, a la me,
a la rú, a la rú, a la me.

No temas al rey Herodes
que nada te ha de hacer;
en los brazos de tu madre
y ahí nadie te ha de ofender.

A la rú, a la me
a la rú, a la me,
a la rú, a la me,
a la rú, a la rú, a la me.

A la rú

Brenda Romero

Go to sleep, lovely Child,
in the arms of love,
while you sleep and rest,
the pain of my sorrow.

A la rú, a la me
a la rú, a la me,
a la rú, a la me,
a la rú, a la rú, a la me.

Don't fear king Herod
for he will do nothing to you;
in the arms of your mother
no one will ever offend you.

A la rú, a la me
a la rú, a la me,
a la rú, a la me,
a la rú, a la rú, a la me.

A la rú

Performed by Brenda Romero

The Matachines dances that are performed by both Pueblo Indians and Hispanos of New Mexico are of obscure origin. In her book *The Matachines Dance of the Upper Río Grande*, Flavia Waters Champe discusses possible origins of both the word and the dances; she indicates that Native Americans and those of Spanish descent both claim these dances as their own. As she points out, Bernal Díaz del Castillo, whose accounts of the conquest of Mexico by Hernán Cortez provide an invaluable insight into the time, likens the dancers of Tenochtitlán under the reign of Montezuma to those dancers of Italy called the *mattacinos.*

The Matachines as they appear in this region, are totally clad, their faces masked, and wear miter-like headgear called *cupiles*. They dance in a stately fashion carrying a *palma,* or short trident-shaped object in the left hand, and a *guaje,* or rattle, held upside down in the right, which is shaken to the beat of the music provided by violin and guitar. They indeed appear otherworldly as they maintain strict adherence to the discipline of the dance. There are those who connect the dance of the Matachines with the dramatization of *Los moros y los cristianos,* which reflects the age of conflict between the Spaniards and the Moors from 711 to 1492, ending with the expulsion from Spain of the last of the Moors as well as the Sephardic Jews. There are also aspects of indigenous Mexican origin that appear in the Matachines pageant.

I believe that the current Matachines tradition of the Río Grande del Norte is a meld of diverse cultural elements of indigenous and European provenance; they may still be evolving within the dynamic patterns of cultural *mestizaje*. This ceremonial dance is performed in the Indian pueblos and in certain of the Hispano villages. I have watched the Tarahumara Indians perform it in the village of Samachique, Chihuahua, in the Barranca del Cobre of northwestern Mexico. There is no doubt that these diverse cultures inhabit distinctly different mythic milieus, yet the Matachines dances are common to all. In the Indian pueblos of the Río Grande del Norte where Matachines dances are performed, the dancers are themselves Indians. Frequently, however, the *músicos* are of Hispano descent.

Larry Torres, a distinguished teacher and scholar who resides in Arroyo Seco, New Mexico, has spent years collecting information regarding the folk dramas of New Mexico. The dance drama still performed in this village is called *Los Matachines*. The version presented here is based on a performance by the villagers of Arroyo Seco, among whom are many members of the extended family of José Damián and Eliza Archuleta, to whom Larry Torres is related. José Damián Archuleta was one of the great traditional *violinistas* of his time. He performed as a Matachines dancer in 1929 in Arroyo Seco, where the pageant was performed again in 1938 and 1985. It is largely through the efforts of Señores Archuleta and Torres that this outstanding version of *Los Matachines* is still a living aspect of the Hispano heritage of Arroyo Seco. It is interesting to note that all of the participants in the Arroyo Seco presentation are of Hispano descent, even though this village is immediately adjacent to Taos Pueblo, where yet another version of the pageant is performed featuring Pueblo dancers and Hispano musicians. Ethnographer Sylvia Rodríguez has studied these presentations as a kind of index of Indo-Hispano relations in Taos; one of the chapters of her recent book deals with the Arroyo Seco Matachines.

The description and interpretation of the dance presented here is based largely on an interview with Larry Torres in his family's living room in Arroyo Seco, New Mexico. Señor Torres reminds us that if there were forty groups of Matachines, there would indeed be forty different interpretations. The cast for the 1987 pageant was sizable and complex. There were twelve Matachines wearing the traditional garb. Señor Torres states that the significance of the number of dancers is open to interpretation; it may represent the twelve apostles, the twelve stations of the cross, the twelve bishops of Rome, the twelve months of the year, or the diverse Indian tribes of Mexico. The number of Matachines varies depending on the community, however; in Arroyo Seco there have traditionally been twelve dancers.

A leading character in the pageant is the figure of *La Malinche,* an extremely complex aspect of the feminine principle. Señor Torres states that the name is derived from Malintzin, the name of

Los Matachines I La marcha

Performed by José Archuleta y Ernesto Montoya

Repeat as appropriate

the Aztec woman who became the translator and consort of Hernán Cortez and who is regarded by Señor Torres and many Mexican thinkers as the mother of *La raza,* the mestizo race that has evolved from the mixture of the Indian and Spanish peoples. *Malinche* is the subject of the novella by Rudolfo Anaya entitled, "The Legend of La Llorona," whose mysterious feminine presence is ubiquitous within the mythos of *La Raza.* (For a further discussion of *La Llorona,* see pp. 108–109.) In the pageant of *Los Matachines,* La Malinche is always portrayed by a preadolescent girl clad entirely in white, thus indicating her purity.

The figure of *El Monarca* also assumes complex proportions. Originally he is thought to have represented the Moorish Prince Selim, who was twenty-two years of age when the Moors were expelled from Spain under the reign of the Sultan Bayezid II. Because of his dynamic personality, his name is still remembered within Hispano tradition, even though he had as yet to attain to the throne at the time. When the related pageant *Los moros y los cristianos* was first performed in Mexico in 1533, the role of Selim was transmogrified in the minds of the Indians into the personality of Moctezuma, thus standing in direct conflict with *La Malinche,* whose own countenance ultimately assumed Christian characteristics. It is fascinating to reflect on the nature of the mythic process that allows for a character to assume more than one aspect at the same time in the mind of the beholder. This is a fine example of the nonlinearity available to one whose mind is actively involved with the portrayal of the myth.

The cast of characters for *Los Matachines* includes *Los Abuelos* (the grandparents), ancestral personages with both positive and negative aspects in the Hispano tradition of the Río Grande del Norte. The countenance of *El Abuelo* inspires fear in the hearts of the Hispanos who as children were convinced that during the summer months, *El Abuelo* might appear and carry them off to the mountains in sacks. During the winter months, the evil shade of *El Abuelo* was shed for a more positive but nonetheless stern countenance that was sometimes seen at Christmas walking around the *luminarias,* bonfires to illuminate the paths of Mary and Joseph to the inn. At this time *El Abuelo* carried a bullwhip and frequently chased children indoors to say their prayers. In several versions of the Matachines pageant, *Los Abuelos* are entrusted with the responsibility of calling the dance steps to the dancers, taking their cue from the *músicos. Los Abuelos* are garbed in old, patched clothing of indeterminate fit. They are grotesquely masked and speak in a weird falsetto, evoking both fear and humor in the minds of the beholders. *El Abuelo* carries his bullwhip, while *La Abuela* has the appearance of being pregnant, thus increasing the sense of the bizarre. The feminine *Abuela* figure also appears at the Arroyo Seco and Taos Pueblo Matachines.

El Toro, the bull, completes the cast of characters, and as the totem animal of Iberia, his presence reflects the Spanish influence on the pageant. *El Toro* wears an animal hide on his back and a horned mask on his head. He lengthens his front legs by holding long sticks in his hands, thereby giving the impression of dancing on all fours.

La *marcha,* or *procesión,* begins as the musicians, one playing the violin, the other playing the guitar, lead the stately line of dancers from the point of origin to the dance area. Following the *músicos* at the head of the procession are the figures of *Malinche* and *El Monarca,* who are in turn followed by the Matachines, with *El Toro* bringing up the rear. The *Abuelos'* positions change in relation to the rest of the figures as they comically draw attention to themselves. The Matachines are striking, mysterious creatures, masked and beribboned, supremely tall in their *cupiles,* which Torres suggests resemble Moorish turbans, the ornate headdress of the Aztecs, or even the bishop's miter. Each of the Matachines carries the *palma* and *guaje.* Torres also suggests that the *palma* may have evolved from the three-pronged spear, or trident, of the Moors. Another interpretation is that

Los Matachines III El Monarca

Performed by José Archuleta y Ernesto Montoya

the *palma* resembles the feathered fan borne by Aztec dancers. Currently the *palma* symbolizes the *Santísima Trinidad,* the sacred Christian trinity. As the procession reaches the dance area, the *músicos* take their seats nearby, and *Malinche* and *El Monarca* go directly to their thrones, from whence they observe the dancing Matachines. *El Toro* takes his place behind the two and occasionally bellows, his raging vociferations gaining in strength and volume as the pageant progresses. The *Abuelos* find some spot in the sidelines, go about adjusting the ribbons of the Matachines, or simply clown about to temper the solemnity of the event.

La Malinche is the title of the second part of the pageant. As the *Monarca* sits on his chair gazing at the spectacle before him, *Malinche,* preceded by the guiding *Abuela,* dances forward in very short steps and in stately fashion between the double lines of Matachines. Meanwhile the Matachines dance in place. At the appropriate times, the *Abuelo* shouts *¡vuelta!* (turn), and the Matachines and the *Abuelo* revolve in place while dancing the proper steps. *Malinche* does not turn, but rather proceeds in her slow fashion to the far end of the two lines of dancers. When she reaches the far end, still guided by the *Abuela,* she slowly turns and begins dancing back to her distant throne. She finally reaches her destination and finds herself standing before and facing the seated *Monarca,* who extends his left hand. *Malinche* slowly blesses the extended hand with the *palma* she holds in her right hand. The pair then slowly revolve their hands around each other in a mysterious exchange of spiritual power and authority. Some scholars believe this moment represents the conversion of Moctezuma. The *Abuela* has, by now, joined the *Abuelo,* and the Matachines have continued to dance in place throughout, always responding to the *Abuelo's* shouts.

The third section is *El Monarca. Malinche* has taken her seat and the Monarca stands facing the corridor separating the two lines of Matachines, his back to *Malinche.* In this spirited dance, *El Monarca* proceeds slowly toward the far end, away from his seat, while all of the Matachines, who mimic *El Monarca's* dance, face his empty throne and the seated *Malinche. El Monarca* finally reaches the far end of the corridor between the Matachines and turns, facing the now distant *Malinche,* and dances back to his original position.

The fourth section of the pageant consists of two parts referred to as *La corona.* In the first part two lines of Matachines face each other, each dancer raising his *palma,* thus forming a canopy beneath which *El Monarca* will dance. This raising of the *palmas* is intended to represent the Matachines' homage to him. Larry Torres suggests that the Matachines represent the Indian tribes of Mexico paying homage to the conquering king of Spain. Whatever the symbolism, it is explicit regarding the sovereignty of *El Monarca.* He dances beneath the canopy to the far end of the corridor, where he turns and slowly returns to his original position. On his return between the dancers, each facing pair of Matachines kneels immediately after *El Monarca* passes them. By the end of this

Los Matachines IV La corona #2

Performed by José D. Archuleta y Ernesto Montoya

part of *La corona,* the two rows are kneeling, facing each other, their *palmas* extended forward and earthward. Their humility is seemingly complete.

In the second part of *La corona,* the Matachines remain kneeling as the *músicos* begin to play the melody for this part of the dance. At this point the power of *El Monarca* is at its greatest, as he slowly dances forward along the corridor between the kneeling figures, hopping over their extended *palmas* in a state of total sovereignty. After reaching the far end of the corridor, *El Monarca* turns and reverses his passage between the dancers. As he passes, the dancers arise, dancing in place, and face in the direction of the thrones where *Malinche* is still seated. When *El Monarca* has returned to the area immediately before the thrones, the dance is complete. It is only after the dancers rise that the *Abuelo* resumes his shouts of *¡vuelta!.* The power of *El Monarca* supersedes his. It is interesting to note that the presence of *Los Abuelos* within the pageant is similar to the presence of *koshares* in many of the Pueblo dances; they serve as clowns whose presence elicits a series of responses that can only be thoroughly understood by an audience whose heritage is imbued with the tradition. The parallels between the figures of *Los Abuelos* and the *koshares* are probably not coincidental.

The fifth section, *La mudada,* also consists of two parts. This dance represents the time of change, a time when *El Monarca* exerts his power over the Matachines. Here *El Monarca,* closely followed

Los Matachines V La mudada #1

Performed by Jose D. Archuleta y Ernesto Montoya

Repeat as appropriate

Los Matachines V La mudada #2

Performed by José D. Archuleta y Ernesto Montoya

by *Malinche*, rearranges the positions of the twelve Matachines by leading each dancer from his original position, displacing the dancer already stationed there, leading the subsequent dancer to the position vacated by the previous dancer. This dance is extremely complex and involves the relocation of all the Matachines. The presence of *Malinche*, who is relegated to a position behind *El Monarca*, implies the involvement of the feminine principle. Torres suggests that the symbolism of this dance may contain aspects of the Moorish attempt to overcome the Christian ethos as Selim, son of the Sultan Bayezid, attempts to fulfill his father's charge to subordinate the Christians through any means, including torture. Torres also suggests that *El Monarca* may be attempting to overwhelm the Indian tribes of Mexico by relocating them in relation to each other. This part of the dance ends as the final dancer is ensconced in his new position and *El Monarca* and *Malinche* are again seated on their thrones.

La mudada, part 2, begins as the Matachines overcome the inertia imposed in the first part and begin to dance themselves back into their original positions, their double columns interweaving in a masterpiece of ancient choreography. All the while *El Monarca* and *La Malinche* observe the dance from their seated positions. Torres suggests that the Matachines might represent the Christians refusing to submit to Selim, who had sought to dominate them. The completion of the other interpretation is that the Indian tribes of Mexico withstood the attempt to dominate them and retained their collective ethnicity. This dance ends when each of the Matachines has returned to his original position.

The sixth section of the pageant is called *La tejida*. This dance involves the weaving of the maypole, which according to Torres has its origins in the European tradition of celebrating the rite of spring in this ancient pagan tradition. It is interesting to note that Taos Pueblo is the single northern Río Grande pueblo found by Champe to incorporate the weaving of the maypole into its own Matachines tradition. Champe also mentions that it has been suggested that the weaving of the maypole is similar to the practice of the Mexican Indian *voladores* of Veracruz, who dive from the top of a very high pole with ropes attached to their ankles and unwind their way to earth from their sky-bound platform.

Los Matachines VI La tejida

Performed by José Archuleta y Ernesto Montoya

At Arroyo Seco the maypole is held in position by *El Monarca* himself, as the dancers weave the intricate pattern of ribbons, each holding the end of a single ribbon, the other end of which is attached to the top of the pole. The top of the pole is also adorned with a bunch of flowers. The first half of the dance involves the weaving of the ribbons, followed by the dancing in place of the Matachines as they look to the top of the maypole. Then there is a slight break in the music, after which the dancers begin to unweave the maypole.

Los Matachines VII El Toro

Performed by José D. Archuleta y Ernesto Montoya

It is interesting to note that the maypole has been incorporated into certain of the Basque sword dances and that *Los Matachines* are associated with the medieval sword dances of Europe, according to some sources. In these instances the *palmas* are regarded as symbolic swords.

The seventh section of the pageant is *El Toro*. Throughout the previous sections, *El Toro* has remained in the background behind the thrones of *El Monarca* and *Malinche*. However, his occasional bellows have gradually increased in intensity, and it is obvious that his presence cannot be ignored. *El Monarca* and *Malinche* are seated on their thrones, and *Los Abuelos* have assumed positions at the far end of the corridor. *El Abuelo* is practicing with his bullwhip, while *El Toro* lunges about between the Matachines, bellowing his rage. As he passes *El Abuelo*, the latter attempts to capture him with his whip, but the first attempts are unsuccessful. Finally the *Abuelo* succeeds in capturing *El Toro*, whom he throws to the ground, overwhelms, and ultimately castrates, jumping to his feet holding *El Toro's* "*huevos,*" or testicles up in the air for all to admire. *El Toro* lies on the ground, defiled, but apparently not dead. Suddenly *La Abuela* registers a moment of excitement, and *El Abuelo* rushes to her fallen form and helps her, as this grotesque old woman gives birth to a rag doll who is then held high for everyone to see.

The eighth dance of the pageant is called *Abuelito de la sierra*. *El Monarca* and *Malinche* remain seated as the *Abuelos* gather their newborn child and with much ado dance their way between the Matachines to the thrones, where they show their baby to *El Monarca* and *Malinche*. They then dance their way back between the two lines of Matachines, who are dancing in place. The melody for this dance is played in the key of G, whereas all of the other melodies throughout the pageant are played in the key of D.

The ninth section of the pageant is *La despedida,* or *La entriega. El Monarca* and *Malinche* leave their thrones and proceed to the opposite end of the double line of Matachines, where they await

Los Matachines VIII Abuelito de la sierra

Performed by José D. Archuleta y Ernesto Montoya

Los Matachines IX La entriega de los Matachines

Performed by José Archuleta y Ernesto Montoya

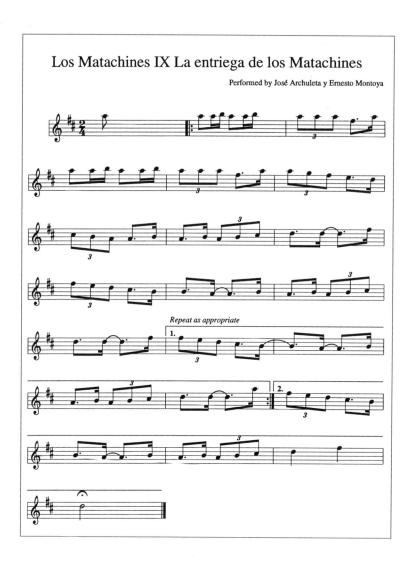

the beginning of the final melody. The musicians begin, *El Abuelo* shouts a final *¡vuelta,!* the entire company turns in place, and the final procession begins, one line of Matachines being led by the *Monarca*, the other by *Malinche*. The two lines proceed in opposite directions for several measures, until they once again dance side by side. The procession trails out of the dance area, led by *El Monarca* and *Malinche* and followed by the Matachines, then *Los Abuelos*, *El Toro*, and finally the *músicos*, who are the last to leave. This dance is sometimes referred to as *La entriega de los Matachines*, because it returns the dancers to the world of nonmythic reality.

The Matachines dances of Arroyo Seco, New Mexico, contain elements common to all such dances as well as elements unique to this community. The music has the simple, beautiful melodies that one associates with *Los Matachines*, but it nevertheless differs from music performed elsewhere. For example the *despedida* to which the dancers march out is totally different from the final *marcha* played in San Juan Pueblo, forty miles to the south. Curiously the *marcha* performed at the pueblo has the same melody line as *La Marcha de los novios*, which I have heard performed by different *músicos* around the Taos area.

It should be reiterated that the interpretation of this presentation of *Los Matachines* is extracted from an interview I conducted with Larry Torres. Wherever this pageant is performed throughout the region of the Río Grande del Norte, people will apply their own interpretations to the meanings of the various components. The actual origins reside in the distant past, when attitudes regarding reality were different from what they are today. One may attempt to intuit the tone of the tradition and then extrapolate meanings, but the conclusions will always remain tentative. And yet the tradition continues to reenact an aspect of the mythic reality of the culture. Whether one can intellectually grasp the meaning of the event is immaterial; participation in the mythic reenactment leads to spiritual transformation. It is this act of transcendence that allows for glimpses beyond a workaday world dominated by economic serfdom.

The performance of *Los Matachines* presented here was recorded in the home of José Damián Archuleta, who was the *violinista*. Ernesto Montoya was the *guitarrista*.

Afterword

I T HAS BEEN FORTY YEARS NOW since I began my wanderings through the American Southwest and Mexico. For most of that time, I have carried a tape recorder with me in order to listen more attentively to the myriad sounds of each locality. I have recorded thousands of songs, conducted hundreds of interviews, and captured the ambiance of many biotic communities on the North American continent.

This has been a humbling and wondrous journey, one that has revealed the importance of curtailing personal cultural biases to avoid filtering my perceptions of other cultures' realities. Long ago it became apparent to me that unless one is born into a culture, one can never fully comprehend its nature. Therefore it is dangerous business for the outsider to openly interpret another culture, inasmuch as points of view may well exist that have no outside equivalent.

Another revelation that came early on was the importance of the natural surroundings in nurturing the evolution of a culture, of invoking the spirit of place in the mind of the beholder. As I have wandered the watersheds of the West, exploring the Columbia and Colorado Plateaus and that other wondrous province of Basin and Range, even following my inclinations deep into the Sierra Madre Occidental and beyond, I have met many fellow humans who have invited me into their communities and allowed me to record their music and their points of view. Thus I have gradually come to understand the enormous importance of cultural diversity, that indeed cultural diversity and biotic diversity are inextricably intertwined. It seems to me that in the human sense, centralization of political power and the imposition of mores from without toll the death knell for human indigeneity and the environment.

As my wife, Katherine and I have traveled through New Mexico and southern Colorado, recording and documenting the folk music of Hispano culture within the watershed of the Río Grande del Norte and beyond, we have witnessed the success of decentralized communities wherein people take care of their own, whose lore hearkens back to a time when the land sustained the physical needs of the community and reciprocity between the people and the land, *la gente y la tierra*, was the basis for an enduring and self-sustaining community of practice. This culture is unique; it appears nowhere else in the world. It has an integrity to be respected, honored and revered. It has a soul.

I cannot possibly express the breadth of my great fortune to have made many friendships within the Hispano culture of the Río Grande del Norte. There are those from within that culture that I count among the dearest friends of my lifetime. Among these dearest of friends is Enrique R. Lamadrid whose contributions to this book and to the understanding of the folklore of this region are supremely valuable. My great friend Cipriano Vigil has devoted his life to the preservation of

Hispano music and has invited me, many a time, to participate in musical adventures throughout the Río Grande del Norte.

My old pal photographer Jack Parsons and I have traveled many a mile together. His photographs of *los músicos* provide great insight into the extraordinary richness of character of *la gente del Río Grande del Norte.*

La música de los viejitos is not a crystallization but rather a presentation from within an ever-evolving musical tradition. It is an expression of musical diversity that reflects a cultural point of view that is itself evolving and that is strong enough to resist domination from without. *¡Viva la gente de la tierra sagrada del Río Grande del Norte!*

Glossary

abuelos   monstrous grandparent figures in the ceremonial dance *Los Matachines*

acequia   irrigation canal

alabado   hymn of praise

alba   dawn song

alegre   happy, joyful

alelí   lily, wallflower

ánima en pena   wandering suffering soul not yet at rest

arenga   harangue, military speech

auto   morality play

bailador/a   dancer

baile   dance, in the sense of both a particular dance and a social event

bandillero   role in Spanish bullfights

bastonero   master of ceremonies (with his cane) at a *baile*

borreguero   shepherd

burro   donkey

Camino Real   the Royal Road from Mexico City to Santa Fe

camposanto   cemetery

canción   song

cancionero   handwritten collection of songs

capullo   flower bud

cautivo/a   captive

chinampa   "floating garden" agriculture

chino/a   curly-haired

chotís/chote   (schottische) couple dance in fast 2/4 time

cibolero   buffalo hunter

ciego   blind

copla   couplet

coro   chorus

corona   crown

corridista   composer and singer of *corrido ballads*

corrido   heroic ballad about tragedy and momentous events

cuadrilla   quadrille

cuando   19th-century ballad form that uses the rhetorical question *¿cuándo?* (when?) to provoke irony.

cuarteta   quartet, four-line verse

cuna   cradle; cradle dance

cupil   mitre-like headgear of Matachines dancers

cutilio   from the French cotillion, the last piece in a set of cuadrillas

décima   Spanish poetic form consisting of the "planta," an introductory verse of four octosyllabic lines, followed by four stanzas of ten octosyllabic lines

despedida   "farewell" stanza

despedimiento   a funeral hymn sung at graveside

disparate   humorous folksong characterized by exaggeration

écossaise   a form of French contredanse

entriega   ceremonial song marking a delivery or rite of passage such as marriage

entriegador/a   singer of an entriega, especially "la entriega de los novios"

estribillo   chorus or refrain

fiesta   feast day

fiesta de los novios   wedding reception

fipple   a plug near the mouthpiece of certain wind instruments, to divert the breath in producing tones

genízaro   detribalized, Hispanicized Indian

gente (del norte)   (Hispano) people (of the north)

guaje   rattle used by Matachines
guitarrista   guitarist
guitarrón   acoustic bass guitar
habanera   a popular late 19th-century song and dance style associated with Havana, Cuba
hermandad   brotherhood
hermano   (*penitente*) brother
hermano mayor   (*penitente*) elder brother
huapango   musical style characteristic of Vera Cruz, Mexico
indita   "little Indian" ballad, or girl
Jornada del Muerto   journey of death
juegos infantiles   traditional children's (musical) games
juglares   medieval court singers
llorona   the Wailing Woman who drowned her children
luminaria   bonfire meant to light the way of Mary and Joseph to the inn at Christmas time
maldición   curse
Malinche   figure representing goodness and feminine purity in the ceremonial dance of *Los Matachines*
mañana   commemorative dawn song
mañanita   celebratory birthday song
mancornadora   an emasculating, deceiving woman
marcha   march
María   Mary
mariachi   style of music from Jalisco, Mexico; also refers to the musical group and the musicians who play it
Matachines   ceremonial dance comprised of Native American an European elements
mentira   "lying" song, tall tale
mestizaje   mixture
monarca   literally the monarch, a figure probably representing a Moorish prince or Moctezuma in the ceremonial dance *Los Matachines*
morada   (*penitente*) chapel
música   music; female musician
músico   male musician
norteño/a   northern
novios   engaged couple; newlyweds
nueva canción   "new song" folk revival
padres   parents, or fathers (priests) of the church
padrinos   godparents
palma   short, trident-shaped object held by Matachines
paño   handkerchief, bandana

penitente   popular, somewhat disrespectful, term for a member of the penitential brotherhood Hermandad de Nuestro Padre Jesús Nazareno (the Brotherhood of our Father Jesus the Nazarene)
peón   peasant, pedestrian
pitero   *pito* player or maker
pito   type of traditional fipple flute (see **fipple**)
placita   small (Hispano) settlement
polka   popular and lively folk dance with roots in 19th century Poland and Hungary
procesión   procession
promesa   holy vow or promise, to God, the Virgin, or the saints
prisionero   prisoner or captive
pueblo   Pueblo Indian or Hispano village
quelite   wild spinach (lambs quarters), also a place name
ranchera   type of popular northern Mexican dance music
redondos   round dances
refrán   refrain
relación   type of humorous folk song characterized by lists of things, people or places
relación aglutinante   form of ballad in which each verse contains an ever-growing list of subjects attached or "glued" to the song
requinto   Mexican treble guitar
romance   Medieval ballad form, ancestor of the modern "*romance corrido*" or *corrido*
rurales   Mexican federal rural police
sala   drawing room or dance hall
schottische   a dance in duple meter, possible ancestor of the chotís
tejida   literally, a weaving action, as in the Maypole section of the Matachines dance
tierra   land
tonada/tonadilla   dance tune or melody
toro   the bull figure in the ceremonial dance *Los Matachines*
tragedia   tragedy
trovador   travelling ballad singer
trovo   contest song, poetic duel
vals/valse   waltz
vaquero   Hispano cowboy
velorio   prayer vigil or wake
verso   verse
viejo   old man
viejos   elders of a community
vihuela   string instrument similar to the guitar
violinista   violinist

Bibliography

Books

Anaya, Rudolfo A. *The Legend of La Llorona.* Berkeley: Tonatiuh- Quinto Sol International, 1984.

Armistad, Samuel G. *The Ballad of Celinos at Uña de Quintana: Essays on Hispanic Literature in Honor of Edmund L. King.* London: Tameis Books, 1983.

Beck, Warren A. and Unez D. Haase. *Historical Atlas of New Mexico.* Norman: University of Oklahoma Press, 1969.

Benedict, Ruth. *Tales of the Cochití Indians.* Washington DC: Smithsonian Institution, BAE Bulletin 98, 1931.

Bernal, Ignacio. *The Mexican National Museum of Anthropology.* Mexico City: 1968.

Bonoratt, Raúl. *Corridos mexicanos.* Mexico: Editores Mexicanos Unidos, 1987.

Braden, Jean. *The Mesilla Valley: A Short History.* Las Cruces, New Mexico:J-Lor Productions, 1982.

Brown, William E. *Islands of Hope: Parks and Recreation in Environmental Crisis.* Washington DC: National Recreation and Parks Association, 1972.

———. *The Santa Fe Trail: National Park Service 1963 Historic Sites Survey.* St. Louis: The Patrice Press, 1990.

Cabeza de Vaca, Alvar Núñez, trans. and ed. by Cyclone Covey. *Adventures into the Unknown Interior of America.* Albuquerque: University of New Mexico Press, 1961.

Cabeza de Vaca Gilbert, Fabiola. *We Fed Them Cactus.* Albuquerque: University of New Mexico Press, 1954.

———. *The Good Life: New Mexico Traditions and Food.1949.* Santa Fe: Museum of New Mexico Press, 1982.

Campa, Arthur B. "Spanish Folksongs in the Southwest." *University of New Mexico Bulletin* (Modern Language Series) 4, 1 1933.

———. *Spanish Folk Poetry in New Mexico.* Albuquerque: University of New Mexico Press, 1946.

———. *Hispanic Culture in the Southwest.* Norman: University of Oklahoma Press, 1979.

Campos, Rubén M. *El folklore y la música mexicana.* Mexico: Publicaciones de la Secretaría de Educación Pública, 1928.

Champe, Flavia Waters. *The Matachines Dance of the Upper Río Grande: History, Music, and Choreography.* Lincoln: University of Nebraska Press, 1983.

Chase, Gilbert. *The Music of Spain.* New York: Dover Publications, 1941.

Cobos, Rubén. "The New Mexican Game of 'Valse Chiquiado'." *Western Folklore,* 15, 2, 1956.

———. *A Dictionary of New Mexico and Southern Colorado Spanish.* Santa Fe: Museum of New Mexico Press, 1983.

Densmore, Frances. *Technique of the Music of the American Indian.* Washington, DC: Smithsonian Institution, BAE Anthropological Papers, 36.

———. *Yuman and Yaqui Music.* Washington, DC: Smithsonian Institution, Bulletin 110, 1927.

———. *Handbook of the Collection of Musical Instruments in the United States National*

Museum. Washington, DC: Smithsonian Institution, Bulletin 136, 1927.

———. *Music of the Santo Domingo Pueblo, New Mexico.* Los Angeles: Southwest Museum Papers, Number 12, 1938.

Díaz del Castillo, Bernal. *The Conquest of New Spain.* Middlesex, England: Penguin Books, 1963.

Dozier, Edward P. *The Pueblo Indians of North America.* New York: Holt, Rinehart and Winston, Inc., 1970.

Espinosa, Aurelio N. *The Folklore of Spain in the American Southwest: Traditional Spanish Folk Literature in Northern New Mexico and Southern Colorado.* Norman: University of Oklahoma Press, 1985.

Fergusson, Erna. *New Mexico, A Pageant of Three Peoples.* Albuquerque: University of New Mexico Press, 1973.

Flores, Jesús Romero. *Corrido de la revolución mexicana.* Mexico: Costa-Amic Editores, 1979.

Free Tract Society. *Cantos de alabanza, pureza y poder.* Los Angeles, 1930.

Geijerstam, Claes af. *Popular Music in Mexico.* Albuquerque: University of New Mexico Press, 1976.

Gonzales, Dolores, ed. *Canciones y juegos de Nuevo Mexico/ Songs and Games of New Mexico.* New York: A.S. Barnes, 1974.

Griego y Maestas, José and Rudolfo A. Anaya. *Cuentos: Tales from the Hispanic Southwest.* Santa Fe: Museum of New Mexico Press, 1980.

Groves Dictionary of Music and Musicians. New York, St. Martin's Press, fifth ed., 1954.

Guerrero, Armando Hugo Ortiz, compilador. *Vida y muerte en la frontera: Cancionero del corrido norestense.* Monterey, Mexico: Hensa Editores, S.A. de C.V., 1992.

Guzmán, Martin Luis. *Memoirs of Pancho Villa.* Trans. by Virginia Taylor. Austin: University of Texas Press, 1965.

Haefer, J. Richard. *Papago Music and Dance.* Manyfarms, Arizona: Navajo Community College and Press, 1977.

Historic Santa Fe Foundation. *Old Santa Fe Today.* Albuquerque: University of New Mexico Press, 1982.

Horgan, Paul. *Lamy of Santa Fe: His Life and Times.* New York: Farrar, Straus and Giroux, 1975.

———. *The Great River.* New York: Holt, Rinehart and Winston, 1977.

Jenkins, Myra Ellen and Albert H. Schroeder. *A Brief History of New Mexico.* Albuquerque: University of New Mexico Press, 1974.

Kennedy, Michael. *The Concise Oxford Dictionary of Music.* Third ed., Oxford: Oxford University Press, 1980.

Kurath, Gertrude Prokosch and Antonio García. *Music and Dance of the Tewa Pueblos.* Santa Fe: Museum of New Mexico Press, 1970.

Lamadrid, Enrique R. "Los Corridos de Río Arriba: Two Ballads of the Land Grant Movement, 1965–70." *Aztlan,* 17, 2 (Fall 1986): 31–62.

———. "Cipriano Vigil y la Nueva Canción nuevomexicana." *Latin American Music Review,* 7, 1 (Spring/Summer1986): 119–222.

———. "Music Straight From the Heart," *New Mexico Magazine,* 66, 7 (July, 1988): 58–63.

———. "Las entriegas: Ceremonial Music and Cultural Resistance on the Upper Río Grande: Research Notes and Catalog of the Cipriano Vigil Collection 1985–87." *New Mexico Historical Review* (January 1990).

———. *Tesoros del Espíritu: A Portrait in Sound of Hispanic New Mexico.* With Jack Loeffler, recordist, and Miguel Gandert, photographer. Albuquerque: Academia / El Norte Publications, 1994.

———. "La indita de San Luis Gonzaga: History, Faith, and Intercultural Relations in a New Mexican Sacred Ballad." In James Porter, ed. *Ballads and Boundaries: Narrative Singing in an Intercultural Context* Los Angeles: University of California Press, 1995: 76–83.

———. "El Sentimiento Trágico de la Vida: Notes on Regional Style in Nuevo Mexicano Ballads": *Aztlán* 22, 1 (spring 1997): 1–21.

———. *Music and Culture on the Río Grande del Norte: the Juan B. Rael Collection of Hispano Folk Music.* Washington, DC: American Digital Library, Library of Congress, American Folklife Center, 1998. (http://memory.loc.gov/ammem/rghtml/rghome.html) Web page includes interpretive essays, biography, bibliography, discography, transcriptions, translations, (more than 200 pp), plus 8 hours of sound files.

Lea, Aurora Lucero-White. *Literary Folklore of the Hispanic Southwest.* San Antonio,

Texas: Naylor, 1953.

———— ed., Eunice Hauskins, and Helene Marau. *Folk-Dances of the Spanish-Colonials of New Mexico*: Examiner Publishing Co., 1940.

Loeffler, Jack. "La Música de los Viejitos." *New Mexico Magazine* (June 1983): 42–48.

————. *Upper Santa Fe Canyon Oral History Project.* Santa Fe: City of Santa Fe, New Mexico 1984.

————. "La Música de los Viejitos: The Hispanic Folk Music of the Río Grande del Norte." 1992 Festival of American Folklife: Smithsonian Institution.

————. "La Música de la gente del Río Grande del Norte/Music of the People of the Northern Rio Grande." *Voices of the West: Songs and Stories of the Land.* The Western States Arts Federation and The Western Folkife Center, 1994.

Marks, Edward B. *Memories of Mexico.* Melville, New York, Music Corporation, 1934.

Martí, Samuel. *Music Before Columbus.* Ediciones Euroamericanas. Klaus Thiele, Gunhild Nilsson, 1978.

————. *Instrumentos musicales precortesianos.* Mexico: Instituto Nacional de Antrpología e Historia, 1968.

McAndrew, John. *The Open Air Churches of Sixteenth-Century Mexico.* Cambridge: Harvard University Press, 1965.

Mendoza, Vicente T. *El romance español y el corrido mexicano.* Mexico: Ediciones de la Universidad Nacional, 1939.

————. *Origen de las canciones.* Mexico: Anuario de la Sociedad Folklórica de México., 1941.

————. *Canciones mexicanas.* New York: Hispanic Institute in the United States, 1948.

————. *Lirica infantil de Mexico.* Mexico: Colegio de Mexico, 1951.

————. *El corrido mexicano.* Mexico: Fondo de Cultura Económica, 1954.

————. *Panorama de la música tradicional de Mexico.* Mexico: Universidad Nacional Autónoma de Mexico, 1956.

————. *La Canción mexicana.* Mexico: Fondo de Cultura Económica, 1961.

Mendoza, Vicente T. and Virginia R. R. de Mendoza. *Estudio y clasificación de la música tradicional hispánica de Nuevo Mexico.* Mexico: Universidad Nacional Autónoma de Mexico, 1986.

Ortiz, Alfonso. *The Tewa World: Space, Time, Being, and Becoming in a Pueblo Society.* Chicago: University of Chicago Press, 1969.

Paredes, Américo. *With His Pistol in his Hand.* Austin: University of Texas Press, 1958.

————. "The Ancestry of Mexico's Corridos: A Matter of Definitions." *Journal of American Folklore* (July-September (1963) 231–235

————. *Folktales of Mexico.* Chicago: University of Chicago Press, 1970.

————. *A Texas-Mexican Cancionero: Folksongs of the Lower Border.* Urbana: University of Illinois Press, 1975.

Parsons, Jack. *Straight From the Heart.* Essay by Jim Sagel. Albuquerque: University of New Mexico Press, 1990.

Pearce, T. M. *New Mexico Place Names.* Albuquerque: University of New Mexico Press, 1965.

Peña, Manuel. *The Texas-Mexican Conjunto: History of a Working Class Music.* Austin: University of Texas Press, 1985.

Rivera, Rowena. "A Fifteenth Century Romance in New Mexico." New Mexico Folklore Record. 15: 80–81.

Robb, John D. *Hispanic Folksongs of New Mexico.* Albuquerque: University of New Mexico Press, 1954.

————. *Hispanic Folk Music of New Mexico and the Southwest: A Self Portrait of a People.* Norman: University of Oklahoma Press, 1980.

Robe, Stanley L. *Hispanic Legends from New Mexico: Narratives from the R. D. Jameson Collection.* Berkeley and Los Angeles: University of California Press, 1979.

Sachs, Curt. *The Wellsprings of Music.* New York: DeCapo Press, 1962.

Sedillo, Mela. *Mexican and New Mexican Folkdances.* Albuquerque: University of New Mexico Press, 1938.

Shaw, Lloyd. *Cowboy Dances.* Caldwell: Caxton Printers, 1952.

Simmons, Merle E. "The Ancestry of Mexico's Corridos." *Journal of American Folklore* (January-March 1963) 1–15.

Sonnichsen, C. L. *Tularosa: Last Frontier of the West.* Albuquerque: University of New Mexico Press, 1960, 1980.

Stark, Richard B. *Music of the Spanish Folkplays in New Mexico.* Santa Fe: Museum of New Mexico Press, 1969.

————. *Juegos infantiles cantados en Nuevo*

Mexico. Santa Fe: Museum of New Mexico Press, 1973.

———. *Music of the 'Bailes' in New Mexico.* Santa Fe: International Folk Art Foundation, 1978.

———. "Notes on a Search for Antecedents of New Mexican Alabado Music." *Hispanic Arts and Ethnohistory in the Southwest,* ed. Marta Weigle. Santa Fe: Ancient City Press, 1983, 117–128.

Toor, Frances. *A Treasury of Mexican Folkways.* New York: Crown Publishers, 1947.

Treviño, Adrian. *Traditional Sayings and Expressions of Hispanic Folk Musicians in the Southwestern United States and Northeastern Mexico.* Vol. I, II, III. Albuquerque: Trellis Publishing Company, 1987.

———. *Hispanic Violin Playing in the Southwest.* Albuquerque: Trellis Publishing Company, 1987.

Van Stone, Mary R. *Spanish Folksongs of New Mexico.* Chicago: R. F. Seymour, 1926.

Vincent, Jenny Wells and Ollie May Ray. *Bailes y Música Para una Fiesta.* Taos, New Mexico: Cantemos Records, 1995.

Weigle, Marta. *Brothers of Light, Brothers of Blood: The Penitentes of the Southwest.* Santa Fe: Ancient City Press, 1976.

Weigle, Marta and Peter White, *The Lore of New Mexico.* Albuquerque: University of New Mexico Press, 1988.

Recordings

Chávez, Alex. *Duérmete Niño and Other Songs.* Albuquerque: University of New Mexico, nd.

———. *El Testamento and Other Songs.* Albuquerque: University of New Mexico, nd.

Glaser, Meg, and Jack Loeffler. *Voices of the West: Songs and Stories of the Land.* Elko, Nevada: The Western Folklife Center, 1994.

Hurricane, Al. *La Prisión de Santa Fe.* Albuquerque: Hurricane Records HS 10026, nd.

Lamadrid, Enrique R. and Jack Loeffler. *Tesoros del Espíritu / Treasures of the Spirit:Family and Faith: A Portrait in Sound of Hispanic New Mexico.* Santa Fe: Museum of International Folk Art, 1989 (compact disks).

Loeffler, Jack. *Music of New Mexico Vol. 1, Hispano Music of the Past.* The Albuquerque Museum. Santa Fe: Peregrine Arts, 1998 (compact disc).

———. *Music of New Mexico, Vol 2, Voices of the Southwest: Selections of Native American and Country Folk Music.* The Albuquerque Museum. Santa Fe: Peregrine Arts, 1998 (compact disc)

Martínez, Roberto. *Tradición y Cultura: Los Reyes de Alburquerque & Los Violines de Lorenzo, Silver Anniversary Album, Fiesta Nuevo Mexicana,* Minority Owned Record Enterprises, LP, n.n., 1987.

Music of New Mexico. *Hispanic Traditions.* Washington DC: Smithsonian Institution/ Folkways, 1992.

Ortiz, Cleofes. *Violinsita de Nueva Mexico.* Albuquerque: Ubik Sound, 1986 (cassette).

Robb, John D. *Spanish and Mexican Folk Music of New Mexico.* Folkways Album FA 2204, New York: Folkways, 1961.

Ruiz, Gregorio. *Música Antigua, con violin y guitarra, por Gregorio Ruiz.* Santa Fe: Kiva Records, 1978 and 1980.

Stark, Richard. *Dark and Light in Spanish New Mexico.* Recorded Anthology of American Music, New York: New World Records, 1978.

Vigil, Cipriano. *Cipriano con la Nueva Canción Nuevamexicana.* El Rito, New Mexico: Compañia de Producciones Musicales, 1985. (cassettc)

Vigil, Cipriano. *Cipriano con Música Folklórica.* El Rito, New Mexico: Compañia de Producciones Musicales, 1994 (cassette)

Vincent, Jenny Wells, collector. Taos 3rd Graders, *A-Be-Ce—El Alfabeto, Se levanta la Niña, and a Mescalero Apache Song,* Americord, 10" LB, CA45–1. 1977.

———. "Trío de Taos: (Hattie Trujillo, Nat Flores, and Jenny Vincent), *Música para una Fiesta,* Cantemos Records, LB reissued with extensive notes, transcriptions, and cassette tape in 1995, CALP ST–121. 1977.

———. Adolfo Frésquez and Tranquilino Lucero, *Piezas Antiguas,* Taos Recordings and Publications, 7" LP, TRP–8. 1975.

———. Cleofes Vigil, *Buenos Días, Paloma Blanca: Five Alabados of Northern New Mexico,* Taos Recordings and Publications, LB, TRP–122. 1970.

———. "Los Charros" (Francisco Vallejos and Rafael Martínez), *Piezas Antiguas,* Taos Recordings and Publications, 7" LP, TRP–8. 1969.

———. Francisco Vallejos and Rafael Martínez,

Bailes de Taos, Taos Recordings and Publications, 7" LP, TRP–6. 1964.

———. Melitón Trujillo, *Taos Spanish Songs*, Taos Recordings and Publications, 7" LP, TRP–2. 1962.

———. Adolfo Frésquez and Tranquilino Lucero, *Taos Matachines Music*, Taos Recordings and Publications, 7" LP, TRP–4. 1962.

———. Jenny Wells Vincent. *Spanish American Children's Songs*, Cantemos Records, 10" LP, CALP–101. 1956.

Films

Hixon, Margaret. *Celebración del matrimonio*, a thirty minute documentary film.

Loeffler, Jack, and Karl Kernberger. *Los Alegres*, a thirty minute documentary film, 1977.

Loeffler, Jack and Jack Parsons. *La Música de los Viejos*, a thirty minute documentary film, 1983.

Loeffler, Jack. *Three Southwestern Vignettes*, a twenty-two minute documentary video. Colorado Springs: Taylor Museum, 1991.

Poling-Kempes, Leslie, and Rhonda Vlasek. *Entre verde y seco/ Between Green and Dry*. A thirty minute documentary film. Santa Fe: Public Media, 1983.

Radio Programs

Loeffler, Jack. *La Música de los Viejitos*, a series of 117 thirty minute radio programs. Santa Fe: Peregrine Arts Studios, 1977–80.

———. *Southwest Sound Collage*, three series totaling fifty-four thirty minute radio programs. Santa Fe: Peregrine Arts Studios, 1984–93.

Loeffler, Jack with Rachel Maurer. *Music as a Symbol of American Pluralism and Identity*, a series of four thirty minute radio programs produced for The Center for the Arts in Society, University of New Mexico. Nancy Uscher, Project Director. Santa Fe: Peregrine Arts Studios, 1998.

Loeffler, Jack and Elaine Thatcher. *The Spirit of Place*, a series of thirteen thirty minute radio programs. Western States Arts Federation. Santa Fe: Peregrine Arts Studios, 1997.

Archives

Jack Loeffler Aural History Archive, Peregrine Arts Studios, Santa Fe, New Mexico.

John D. Robb Archive of Southwestern Music, University of New Mexico, Albuquerque, New Mexico.

Index